WHAT'S BEHIND YOUR STAMPS:

The Post Office Story

Published by Godzchild Publications
a division of Godzchild, Inc.
22 Halleck St., Newark, NJ 07104
www.godzchildproductions.net

Printed in the United States of America 2017 - 1st Edition

Library of Congress Cataloging-in-Publications Data
WHAT'S BEHIND YOUR STAMPS: Post Office Story/Ventnor T. Wright

ISBN 978-1-942705-43-7 (pbk.)

1. Wright, Ventnor T. 2. Inspirational 3. Purpose 4. Self-Help
5. Post Office 6. Community

2017

TABLE OF CONTENTS

THANKYOU

I must give a thank you to the several postmasters with whom I was fortunate to work. They were kind and obliging to me as I ran and operated my own funeral home business fourteen out of the twenty-five years that I was employed by the post office. I would not have been able to do so without their understanding. Of course, my primary responsibility was making sure I took care of my postal responsibilities first, as the Post Office "paid my bills and put food on my table." It also enabled me to provide for my family while I built my business.

Special thanks to the last postmaster I worked with. She was very understanding and obliging in letting me leave work early, or take days off, when needed, as long as I got my work done. That was a huge help. I always said that God gave me favor with my bosses, and it made my job as a supervisor more palatable. So sincere thanks to you all, **especially to "Meghyn"** (If you're reading this, you know who you are), for under your tutelage I grew as a person, and though you may not have realized it, you helped me to serve my funeral home customers because of your understanding. Thank you "Meghyn."

I also need to thank, a past fellow employee, Martha, for, one day saying "someone should write a book about this place." Martha, a friendly but tough woman who could handle herself, worked as a "mailman" at the post office where I first was employed. I happened to be in earshot of Martha that day when she suggested that. She said it sarcastically, just blurting it out, but her suggestion hit home with me. That particular morning was a typical work day, filled with humor, drama, and postal chaos. Unknowingly, she planted the seed in me to one day write a book of the postal experience.

And last but not least I thank my wife, Leslie, who upon reading the first, oh I guess fifty pages, said, "I like your story, it sounds good honey"! She encouraged me by saying that. She gave suggestions, helped with editing, and as a wife, provided the necessary constructive criticism. Thus, here we are.

INTRODUCTION

It is my personal belief that the public has little knowledge and understanding of what goes on in the Post Office or how the postal mail system functions. These things are written that the public would have an understanding, of how the Post Office operates; to know how the mail gets from one point to another, and the individuals that make it happen on a daily basis. You will also get a glimpse into personalities, attitudes, and lives of the personnel that work within the system.

In my twenty-five years of being employed by the Post Office, I have worked at various locations, four to be exact. Some offices operated better than others mostly due to the quality of local management, and the quality of the employees. That being said, the location and names of the actual employees and managers I worked with have been changed to protect their identities. Many of the conversations remain true, and the personalities are consistent with the individuals I encountered. However, some things have been added to hopefully compliment the overall writing.

The Post Office carries with it a somewhat military managerial style environment. The employee/labor relations manual insists that "employees are to obey instructions of their supervisor." Hence there's a natural opposition in effect. Employees don't like being told what to do unless the instruction takes the responsibility off of them, or it benefits them in some way, and in that case they will say "just tell me what you want me to do so I can do my job…I just want to do my job." As far as the work environment, there was a fair amount of backstabbing at almost every level within the post office. However, because of my position as a "Front Line" supervisor, I mostly experienced such behavior among the clerk and mail carrier crafts.

The setting is a suburban post office workroom floor, containing a "P.O. Box section," a clerk processing and distribution area, and a mail carrier function. There is also a customer lobby with a sales area aka the "retail window". Most Post Offices are open Monday through Saturday for business; however, the actual work week starts on a Saturday and runs through Friday.

In closing, I would like for you the reader to keep in mind that the setting for this writing is a postal, blue collar work environment. Some of the conversations and circumstances in this book may contain language that might prove to be offensive. So please accept my apologies in advance.

CHAPTER **ONE**

DAY ONE, Wednesday

0300: My alarm clock goes off, and as the man in the old "Dunkin' Donuts" commercial would say, it's "time to make the donuts". I slowly roll out of bed; I must, because I get vertigo if I get up too fast. Once standing, I then walk to the bathroom. I read my daily bible scripture, wash up, and get dressed. I then walk over to the couch, kneel down and pray. Before I leave I walk over to my wife, who's in bed asleep, lean over to kiss her on her forehead and tell her that I love her. Sometimes she will move and nod her head as if to say yes. Other times she'll remain asleep and later that day will say "I don't remember you leaving this morning. Did you say goodbye to me?" Heading out, I begin my drive to work.

0345: Samantha stops at the local convenience store to get her bottle of soda…her caffeine fix.

0350: At the Post Office, the first two of three distribution clerks pull into the driveway as they arrive to work. They notice that the fence gates are still chained with the lock on it and that one car is missing. So they both get out of their cars to unlock and open the chained fence gates, park their cars with the front of the cars facing outward, enter the building, disarm the alarm, walk into the women's locker room, do their thing, and finally clock in at 0400 hours. Transportation truck number one, which typically would have arrived prior to the first clerks, arrived at the same time as the two clerks, with a quarter truckload of mail and packages. Such a load amount is typical.

0400: Upon clocking in, the distribution clerks begin the day by unloading the mail from the truck. The truck typically arrives at the same time as the clerks. The unloading of the truck takes about five to seven minutes depending on the amount of mail. Once unloaded, the truck pulls away from the dock and makes it way back to the plant for the next transportation trip which should arrive in about another hour and a half, about five thirty A.M.

0405: Clerks begin their daily routine of casing/sorting the letter and flat mail as well as sorting the parcels. One clerk for each function; one clerk cases the letters, another cases the flats and breaks down magazines/catalogs, and another sorts the packages also known as parcels. Packages may be smaller in size and lighter in weight than parcels. Parcels tend to be larger in size and generally weigh over two pounds.

Now when a clerk cases or sorts mail, they do so by grabbing a stack of letters, large envelopes or magazines, depending on what mail is to be processed first, and places them in either their left hand or left arm. They then will, with their right hand, grab an item, one piece at a time, read the address, and then place it onto a boxed shelf or pigeon hole like box. The pigeon hole like box represents a particular delivery route, whereupon residents live, and it will have a route number assigned to it. If a particular address or company gets a lot of mail the clerk will throw the mail into a single bin or white box like tub deemed specifically for that address. The process for sorting packages or parcels is very similar except the items are thrown or tossed into a suspended canvas bag, or canvas hamper on wheels. So basically, the clerk sorts the various types of mail to the proper route, based on the address, and the mail carrier aka "mailman," will sort the mail into smaller bins or address slots based on the street and house number. Such slots may be one to two inches in width.

An experienced clerk or mail carrier's hand, after weeks or even months of getting familiar with a pigeon hole like wall, will upon reading the address, automatically extend to the appropriate bin or address slot virtually without thought. However, with time, some clerks and even mail carriers, unfortunately, will learn to slow down the sorting of mail just to extend the process or time. Why, you may ask? It is because they are paid by the hour, not by the piece. Another type of postal employee called a Rural Carrier, whom we shall introduce later on, gets paid by the piece and type of mail items, and a number of deliveries or addresses on their particular route as opposed to getting paid by the hour. Anyway, let's move on with the production.

0407: Telephone rings, maybe two or three times, and it's within these early morning hours of the day that no one really wants to answer the phone because it's generally not a good call or call you want to hear. Nevertheless, Bitsy walked over to the supervisor desk and answered the phone. The other clerk, Samantha, stopped working and turned to follow Bitsy with her eyes, as she walked by, watching and listening. It was distribution clerk Pudgy calling.

"Good morning Creeks Bend Post Office Bitsy speaking."

"Hi Bitsy, this is Pudgy."

Bitsy paused and rolled her eyes.

"I'm calling out sick today. I will not be into work…I have a migraine."

"Okay," said Bitsy deliberately, "I will let Mr. V know. I hope you get to feeling better soon."

So Bitsy hung up the phone and the other clerk, Samantha also rolled her eyes, as Bitsy proceeded to say "I knew she was going to call out. I just had that feeling that Pudgy was going to call out sick today. You know her favorite baseball team played last night, and you know she likes to stay up late to watch the game, and then will call out the next day claiming she has a migraine. It's like clockwork…boy, I can't believe her!"

"Well, why doesn't management do something about her, you know Bitsy? I mean it's so predictable," stated Samantha.

"Well, what can they do Samantha? I mean, they can't touch her because she has an FMLA approved medical condition, you know Samantha, the Family Medical Leave Act! Once somebody gets on that there's not much management can do. As long as the person doesn't exceed their monthly frequency rate they're virtually untouchable. And management has to be very careful how they handle those situations, especially if they try to take disciplinary action against her," responded Bitsy. "Heck, she could sue them and she would probably win!"

"Yeah, wow, I guess you're right. Geez Bitsy, that's like giving a person a license to call out sick! Whenever they don't feel like coming in to work they just call out using their FMLA. I mean I know there are some people who really do qualify for FMLA but I'm sure there are a lot who really don't have a legit condition and therefore they abuse it!"

"Yeah, I know, Samantha. Uhhh, I'm so sick of these people, I can't wait until I retire, exclaimed Bitsy."

"What's holding you back Bitsy, Samantha asked?'

"Well, I guess I could retire now," she responded, "because I have the age and the years but I would still have to wait until I reached sixty-two to collect social security. Besides, I have some financial issues that I want to get rid of before I retire."

"Yeah, I hear ya. Well, you better not retire yet Bitsy, at least not while I'm still here...I need you here!"

Bitsy, as the two employees return back to sorting the mail, writes down on a piece of paper the amount of mail, and issues, to give me when I arrive. She knows I don't like hearing about the bad stuff like people calling out or problems with the mail, especially first thing in the morning, so she finds it easier to tell me by writing the details down on a piece of paper. The truth is I don't like hearing it or reading it. I guess I'm really not cut out for being a supervisor in the post office. The supervisor gets all the complaints. Everybody wants to dump on the supervisor.

Pudgy a divorcee, I call her Pudgy because of her build, is a short chubby lady, approximately 67 yrs old, gets "migraines" and therefore calls out about 5 times per month. She doesn't necessarily like taking orders but if you use some psychology with her you can usually get her to do the work. She also seems to work better when Bitsy is not around. Pudgy for some reason no longer likes Bitsy anymore. From what I hear, they used to be real close friends. I think Bitsy eventually got tired of Pudgy constantly calling out sick when she really wasn't, you know like working the system? Bitsy once said to me that any time Pudgy's favorite professional sports team plays a televised night game, she's sure to call out sick the next day. Anyway, Pudgy really needs to retire but like so many employees in the post office she can't afford to do so. Most employees, because of the amount of overtime they work, get used to the extra money and therefore live above their means.

She, Pudgy, will usually approach me with an issue or two saying "Mr. V, I have a situation." It's often due to the amount or volume of letters she has to sort. So she'll begin venting about the possible scenarios that could arise during the morning processing of mail and how the plant keeps sending us the mail in certain conditions. Some letters will be placed in the trays with the addresses upside down and others placed in the same tray with the addresses facing backward. Ideally, the letters should be placed into the trays right side up with the addresses all facing the same direction. So, I will listen and say "Ok I will get back to you," or I may say, "Okay I'll call the plant." Then I'll walk away shaking my head. It's like, EVERYDAY she has a freaking issue or complaint.

0410: The sorting of mail continues. The two clerks are talking to each other about family issues. They also talk about the post office and recent changes involving the downsizing of the clerk craft. Some clerks are made to cross over to the carrier craft or relocate to another location miles, even hours away, or else lose their postal jobs.

I, the A.M. Supervisor, Mr. V, pull into the local convenience food store to get my daily bag of their Thin Style pretzels, and a bottle of their Mango flavored Iced Tea. Once you become a part of the "postal family" just about everything you do becomes routine, habitual, like clockwork. So I head to the checkout counter, say my daily good morning to the cash register clerk, exchange a brief conversation, and we wish each other a good day. I walk to my car, open the door, sit down onto the driver seat, fasten my seatbelt, push the ignition button, undo the parking brake, put the gear selector into drive, pull out of the parking lot, and continue driving to work. Like I said, everything is routine!

So, back at the post office, the conversation goes like this…"Well, you know Bitsy," said Samantha, "everything around us is changing, like it or not it seems to be what's happening anymore. Thank god for the post office, huh? I mean if this were typical corporate America we might not have that option…you know?"

"Yeah, I guess you're right Samantha. It's like we constantly complain about this place but really, where would we be without the post office? I mean most of us hate it here but you know what…we won't leave…we need the check…we need the benefits. Try finding that outside of here."

"Yeah, I know… you can't," said Samantha."

0415: I, A.M. Supervisor Ventnor, pull into the postal parking lot next to where the early morning mail processing clerks park. I noticed that one of the early clerks, Pudgy's, car is missing and I shake my head because I kinda know the deal. Anyway, I back up my car looking only looking into the rearview and side view mirrors just as I was taught in my early postal years as a mailman. Before I get out of my car I close my eyes and pray as is my custom, "Well, Heavenly Father here we go again, You and me, into this place. Thank You that I made it here safely once again and that I have a job, I may not like it, but I have a job so that I can provide for my family. I pray that I will have the resources and proper staffing to get the mail delivered in a safe and timely manner. Help me to make sound decisions. I also pray that I will not be a pain or burden to my boss, Meghyn. Thank you for hearing me. In the name of Jesus, I pray, amen.

So I, A.M. Supervisor Ventnor, "Mr. V," as I'm called by the employees, walk up to the rear platform single door. I stick the copper colored key into keyhole, walk up to the next single door, unlock it, walk over to the time clock where the employee badges are stored, swipe my yellow colored supervisor timecard and officially clock in. Again, it's routine.

I'm a fifty-three year old, Black man with twelve years of experience as a frontline postal supervisor under my belt and twelve years as a mail carrier prior. Add that up and I have been a postal employee for twenty-four very long years. I'm known as a sharp dresser and have become accustomed to sporting a tie-it-yourself bow tie. Besides working at the Post Office, I also own and operate my own funeral home and cremation service. I guess you could say that I "burn the candle at both ends of the stick."

I'm not the stereotypical postal supervisor. But because I know I still need the job, as I have not yet qualified for retirement, and because of the work ethic I learned from my father, I press my way through the demands of the position. By nature, I'm a caring and supportive type person, yet over time I've learned to hate the people I supervise. Someone once told me that "When the job starts changing you into someone you don’t want to be that’s when it will be time for you to quit.” Well, as for me, I had reached that point a long time ago; it’s just that I can’t retire yet.

Because of the bow tie, some of the employees call me “Hurricane Schwartz” as in the Philadelphia area television weatherman personality. It seems nearly everyone in the office has a nickname. Anyway, I walk in and immediately exclaim “Hip hip hooray she’s not here today.”

I had already assumed that Pudgy probably was not here because I had noticed when I pulled into the parking that her car was nowhere to be seen.

Bitsy and Samantha begin to chuckle and repeated saying, “Yeah, hip hip hooray she’s not here today!” Just like that, the atmosphere changed, or at least it did for a moment. A few of the distribution clerks don’t like working with Pudgy because they think she’s lazy and paces herself to get help later on during the processing phase… saving the work so to speak…they call it “job security.”

Bitsy, as we call her, also because of her size, is a fifty-eight-year-old divorcee, stands at 5’3” tall and weighs about ninety-five pounds soak n’ wet. After work, she can be seen running three to five miles a day. The running helps her to deal with the stress of the job and her home life. She has her two daughters and four granddaughters living at home with her. Apparently, neither daughter gives her any money towards helping with the utilities or the mortgage. The two daughters once lived on their own but eventually returned back home.

Bitsy has enough years of service, thirty-five, and the age, fifty-eight, to retire but won't due to her housing the grandchildren and helping her two daughters out financially. She always says, "as soon as I can leave this place I'm out of here…these people drive me crazy. I've known Bitsy for eight years now and she's been saying that ever since.

Pound for pound, Bitsy is probably the hardest working, and most cooperating postal employee that I've ever met. The more you talk about how hard she works the harder and faster she will work. She thrives on it. Oddly enough, she happens to be the clerk union shop steward. She even complains about being in that position. Most shop stewards aren't as friendly or as helpful as Bitsy is and rarely possess such a work ethic as she does. Bitsy, with her all systems ahead personality, just wants things to operate smoothly and in an efficient, productive and timely manner. Her motives are unselfish and are governed by what will work best for the office.

Knowing that I'm not a morning person, the second I clock in, Bitsy, without saying good morning or some kind of greeting, will give me the "four-one-one" on what's happening. Oh, how I hate that moment. It's like a heavyweight being thrown upon me as soon as I walk thru the doors.

Anyway, Bitsy proceeds by saying…"I'm sorry Mr. V, I know you don't like to hear this stuff first thing in the morning when you arrive but I thought you should know."

I hate hearing that phrase, "I thought you should know." So, I take a deep breath and then begin listening as Bitsy starts to tell me about the large volume of mail that has arrived this morning from the plant. She'll also add a dose of complaining about the postmaster and how she violates the postal/clerk union contract. How does she violate the postal/clerk union contract you ask? Well, one way she does it is by using non-clerk employees, such as mail carriers, to do clerk work. She would rather pay out on a grievance settlement as opposed to calling in or scheduling in an extra clerk. The clerks love it when she violates the contract and has to pay out grievance monies because they look at it as free money.

Strangely enough, even though Bitsy represents her fellow employees through the union, she complains about them more than management does. It's almost as if she's ratting them out, and yet at the same time represents them. Nevertheless, Bitsy almost always gives a suggestion or two on what to do in light of the situation. Now I don't mind it as much when someone complains yet will also have a solution. Usually, I will take her advice and will say "Okay that's fine." Hey, if someone else has the answers, such as a better way of accomplishing a task, already figured out, then why should I waste mental energy racking my brain, especially if I can come out smelling like a rose?

0432: I proceed to the scanner room to check and to make sure that all of the handheld scanners have downloaded the previous day's scans. Scanning has become a vital element in the shipping business. Customers want to know where their packages and mail pieces are, and when the expected date and time is. The proper and timely scanning of such items enables the customer to follow their item's journey. All the customer has to do is enter the item or tracking number provided them by the post office into their home computer or smartphone, and voila! They have the information at hand. Now there will be times when the tracking information won't be obtainable due to perhaps the retail clerk or mail carrier failing to properly scan the item in upon receipt from the customer. Sometimes, it may simply be a download issue within the system itself. However, most times the information would be available.

0434: I do my daily walk through the post office workroom and retail lobby areas to check for any undelivered mail. There better not be any such mail or heads will fly! No, absolutely ***no*** carrier or postal employee, including local management is authorized to delay mail, especially first class or preferential type mail. You must obtain permission, preferably in writing, to do so. And you better have a sure 'nuff darn good explanation why you need to delay the mail.

I also look for any missed collection mail from the previous day, a BIG No No! This is mail which was either collected by the mail carriers from their customers while they were delivering mail or from postal customers that actually brought the mail pieces into the post office themselves. I have seen employees, management, in particular, loose their jobs over such incidences. Craft employees, clerks, and carriers, love it when managers are disciplined, or loose their jobs.

I then inspect all the newly arrived morning mail, and color code all bulk rate standard mail for proper day's arrival and delivery date depending on its time of arrival to the office. If bulk rate standard mail arrives on Wednesday it must be delivered no later than Friday. It's a two-day cycle. Basically, bulk rate mail is any non-first class or preferential mail. I was taught a long time ago by my old postmaster to "always inspect what you expect." Therefore a concerned and responsible supervisor or postmaster will inspect the building, mail bins, and any equipment stored on the loading docks before leaving the post office at the end of the workday. They will also inspect all postal delivery vehicles driven by the mail carriers just to make sure that no mail was left behind in the mail trucks.

0440: I gather the clerk employees and go over their duties & responsibilities for the rest of the distribution and processing portion of the morning. I will also utilize this time to address any issues of employees not working together as a unit. However today I will skip that exercise simply because Bitsy and Samantha are responsible and knowledgeable workers. If I were to give them such a speech they would simply say "Mr. V save your breath we know our jobs." They're right; they do!

0445: I arrive at the supervisor desk. The supervisor's desk is stationed right in the middle of the workroom floor, strategically positioned in the middle of the clerk and carrier function areas. The carrier cases are lined up on one side of the room while the clerk distribution area is lined up on the other side of the floor. Behind this processing area lies the retail window section which is partitioned off from the clerk and carrier operation by a non-weight bearing wall. The wall is designed to keep the public from seeing the mail processing area as well as minimizing any noise produced by the carrier and clerk employees, such as bad language. Hey, I hate to say it, but it's basically a blue collar job with blue collar mentality workers.

I then arrange and organize the previous day's paperwork, and clean up any and all cluttered paperwork left behind by the closing P.M. supervisor. Lastly, I will reload the printer with a fresh ream of paper. Now my desk is clean. To function at my best, I need a clean clear desk.

After that, I will make sure all attempted packages from the previous day have a scanned label and sheet attached to them indicating and verifying that the package was handled properly according to Standard Operating Procedures (SOP). This may take fifteen minutes or so.

Once that is completed, I then, as supervisor, log into the vehicle daily maintenance system to make sure that the mail carriers properly entered the beginning and ending mileages and correct vehicle numbers. If a carrier consistently fails to input the daily vehicle information into the system, the Vehicle Maintenance Facility at the plant will assume that the truck is not being used and therefore not needed. The end result could be a loss of that mail truck for the office. Of course, corrective disciplinary action may be taken against the employee that fails to properly input that particular vehicle's information. Not good! Every route must have a mail truck.

During this time of the morning, the clerk employees will carry on various conversations be they job related or that of a personal nature. You can learn a lot about people as they share and talk about their personal preferences and or issues.

I can hear Bitsy and Samantha talking. Bitsy's flat case and Samantha's letter case are right next to each other so it's easy for them to carry on a conversation. Samantha is talking about her daughter.

"Hey, Bitsy, said Samantha, you will not believe what my daughter asked me last night!"

"What Samantha?" responded Bitsy, "What did she ask you…for the keys to the car?"

"On this particular occasion, I wish she had asked me for the car. No, she asked me if her father and I had sex before we were married! Oh, I was so caught off guard. I mean she and I have talked about the, you know, birds and the bees but never about her father and I."

"Well, Samantha she is seventeen and you know how teenagers are these days," replied Bitsy.

"I know Bitsy, I know she's seventeen and I'd really like for her to feel that she could ask me anything but that was too much of a personal question for me." responded Samantha.

"So what did you tell her," asked Bitsy?"

"Well, nothing…I mean what could I say…I kinda froze, you know? For a moment it felt like my face had turned as red as an apple."

"Knowing you Samantha I can imagine. You know everybody thinks you're Miss Goodie Two Shoes anyway, responded Bitsy."

"Oh, yeah right…come on Bitsy!"

"I'm sorry Samantha I was just kidding. But you do have that reputation," stated Bitsy. "Soooo, tell me, what did you say to her?" asked Bitsy.

"I mean sure her father and I had premarital sex. But I was out of high school by that time."

"So what, are you saying that it's okay to have premarital sex once you're out of high school?" asked Bitsy.

"No no no. That's not what I meant. I guess it's really just that I didn't want her to think it was okay, you know what I mean Bitsy?"

"That what was okay?" asked Bitsy.

"You know, that it was okay to have sex before getting married. Really Bitsy, you KNOW I was raised Catholic. I mean strict Catholic. Heck, I would NEVER have asked my mother that question. First of all, my mother would have slapped the crap out of me for even asking her such a private and personal question. Secondly, we just didn't talk about things like that. I mean my parents were not that transparent with us especially about sex. I was the only girl out of five children. It's like had I told my daughter that we did have premarital sex it would be like saying 'Oh sure it's okay!' I mean that's how I think she would have interpreted it." responded Samantha.

"Oh, come on Samantha, you don't know that. You probably missed out on a good opportunity to open up and to relate to your daughter. I wish I could have had conversations like that with my daughter's." stated Bitsy.

"I mean her father and I were committed to each other. We knew we were gonna get married. We loved each other, at least at that time in our lives. Plus it seems we were more mature for our age back then than the kids of today, you know what I mean Bitsy. I mean the kids of today Bitsy! Come on!" exclaimed Samantha.

"Yeah, I know what you mean," Bitsy answered. "But I still think you could have opened up to her."

"Yeah, I guess you're right Bitsy. Well, maybe she will ask me again."

"I don't know Samantha, I think you missed out on a golden opportunity."

0500 - 0510: Begin uploading the Delivery Operations System (DOS) on the computer. DOS is available everyday at five o'clock AM to pull or download the previous day's daily reports to evaluate the carrier's performance. Some reports are redundant having the same information as another report. But still, we have to pull all of them. Upper management, at the district level, can tell if you fail to pull all of the reports. They believe you're not managing if you don't upload and print them out. Because of technology, everything is connected…and everything is seen by "big brother."

Just to note, I will refer to various postal systems, and use a slight variation of names due to let's say copyright, trademark, or infringement rights. Such systems, such as DOS and TAAS, actually exist but again in a slight variation, so I will attempt to maintain their "secrecy" by slightly changing the name or acronym.

It is also at this point that the other distribution/retail window clerk arrives to work and clocks in. Her name is "CeeDee" which is short for Chanzhou Dwongxhi. CeeDee, a forty-year-old married woman, is of Chinese descent. She is a sickly person but that doesn't stop her from being a good worker, as long as she reports to work. I think she's often ill because being born in China and after coming to the United States she never obtained proper vaccinations as a child. Therefore she is susceptible to anything; namely infections. She is also a breast cancer survivor. CeeDee's biggest problem as far as being an employee is her attendance and tardiness.

Once CeeDee came out of the ladies room I yelled across the floor saying, "Okay people you know the drill…flats and letters done first. Parcels and spurs can wait 'til later. The carriers need mail to case. We don't want the carriers waiting for mail, it's not productive. The carriers must have enough mail at their cases when they arrive or upper management will push back their starting times back claiming the carriers, when they clock in, do not have a sufficient amount of mail to work with."

"Okay Mr. V," they reply back to me, "you're the boss!"

"Yeah, right I'm the boss. Everybody knows I'm not the boss… upper management is the boss. I'm just a messenger, caught in the middle."

"Well, Mr. V," replied Bitsy, "we think you're a good messenger. But you're not like your uncle!"
"Ha ha ha, oh boy thanks!"

When Bitsy was first hired by the post office she worked under my uncle, the postmaster at the time. I remember telling my uncle about Bitsy because he knew she was still working in the post office, as well as our office. He thought she was one of the best employees he had ever hired. In fact, he would often tell me that Bitsy would run circles around me if we ever had a contest. Bitsy said he used to refer to her as Half Pint with a ton of heart.

"Hey, Mr. V?" yelled Bitsy, "When I first began working in the post office, and for your uncle Carl, he made it a point to let me know he was the boss. You know your uncle Mr. V, didn't take any mess from anybody…not even from upper management. Heck, I remember once when someone from the district had come out to the office to observe the operation. Your uncle had thrown the person off the floor and made him leave. I think the guy was citing the office for lack of supplies in the lobby area. Heck, I even remember your uncle pressing his finger into a carrier's chest one day because he thought the carrier was talking too much. I think the carrier would stop casing mail so he could tell his stories."

"Yeah, back in those days management could do that kind of stuff and get away with it. Today you would probably lose your job." I responded.

"Thank God things have changed." quipped Samantha. "Although there are a few people who I would like to stick my finger into."

0510: Telephone rings. *Oh, boy here we go,* I say to myself. Usually, when the phone rings this early it's an employee calling out sick or with some sort of emergency. Nevertheless, I proceed to answer the phone with a sedated like voice.
"Good morning, Creeks Bend post office, Mr. V speaking may I help you?" (It's a mail carrier calling out sick).

"Yes, this is Monique, I'm calling out sick and I will not be in today."

Monique is a single Black woman with two daughters. As a temporary status employee on the carrier side, she is looking to becoming a regular carrier with full-time benefits.

So I ask, "What's wrong Monique"?

"I don't feel well and I have a terrible headache…I just can't come in today."

"Well, how about if you came in and just cased up a route and I will have someone else deliver it and you can go home early?"

"No!"

This sick call is next to the employees scheduled day off this week so I proceed as follows

"By the way Monique, I notice you are scheduled off tomorrow, right?"

"Yes, I am…listen Mr. V, I said I'm sick, I feel nauseous and I'm too sick to come into work. I will not be coming in today."
I press her again, "So you are refusing to come into work today?"

Again she stated rather angrily, "I said I'm sick. I'm not coming in. I'm calling out sick. What part of that don't you understand?"

Continuing to push for an answer I ask, "Hmmm, didn't you previously submit a leave slip for this day but it was denied because the calendar was full with carrier's already approved to be off?"

Monique, with more of an attitude, then responds, "So now you're harassing me? Listen Mr. V you do what you have to do. I'm sick and I'm not coming in." The phone suddenly goes click.

I then say to myself, *It's amazing how often employees get sick next to their scheduled day off, or next to a holiday.* Anyway, this is the second time in two weeks that this particular employee has called out sick next to her scheduled day off. Hence she has established a pattern of calling out. Furthermore, as I had mentioned, this employee had previously requested to be off on this particular day but the request was denied.

Well, since she hung up so fast I made an effort in calling her back to inform her that I would need a doctor's note from her stating that she was incapacitated for duty and therefore unable to work. However, the phone rang and eventually the answering machine came on so I was only able to leave a voicemail.

(Occasionally, based on the individual's sick leave usage or emergency call outs, I will proceed to ask for a doctor's note from an employee and informing them that they will be required to provide medical documentation upon their return to work indicating their inability to work. Especially if it's a situation such as the one previously mentioned.)

0514: I document the call/conversation and then proceed to fill out postal form Employee Leave Request Sheet for the employee calling out. I simply go into the Time and Attendance System (TAAS) and enter eight hours of unscheduled sick leave (USL) for them. Now, when I input her sick leave request into the timekeeping system, it will also notify the folks down at the district level regarding her multiple unscheduled absences. The folks at the district level will then send us out an email alert indicating an employee's attendance record. I or any manager will be held responsible to take any corrective action needed. If we don't then my superior and I could have corrective action taken against us, although usually, it's me. So, when Monique does report to work I will perform a Pre-disciplinary Investigation (PDI) with her due to the nature of the call, especially since she had previously requested that day off, and the fact that she has established a pattern of unscheduled sick calls.

0518: I return to doing DOS to finalize pulling yesterday's paperwork. Then begin entering carrier employee's names into the system according to their daily assignment. Next I enter the volume amount of the pre-sorted bulk rate catalogs which had been placed at the carrier's cases yesterday afternoon after the carriers had left for the street to deliver their mail.

0520: Now clerk Samantha, another divorcee, despite being an all-around good employee, is known to be an instigator and a gossiper. She knows the distribution and processing system very well as she was once an Acting Supervisor at a different location years ago. Samantha is a single mother with two high school children. She doesn't use much vacation time but likes to take Saturdays off when she can, to go out of town and spend time her boyfriend. Now I must say that Samantha is a bit of a complainer and a slight "worry wort."

When she asks…"Mr. V what are we going to do if someone calls out or if Meghyn moves me to another operation…what will we do?"

"Samantha, everything will work out, stay calm, the job will get done," is my usual response.

"Yea your right Mr. V, it always works out."

Boy, I say to myself, *Geez, do I have to be a "head shrink" around this place too!*

Samantha can usually be found sorting parcels or working wherever needed. Occasionally, the office will receive containers of live insects, or baby chicks peeping away, or some sort of live creature such as honey bees. This morning, she scans such a package as

'Arrived at Unit' and then brings it over to me. Placing the container on my desk…"Mr. V, we have a package of baby chicks that have just arrived. I already scanned them 'Arrived at Unit' so now you have to call the customer and let them know their package is here."

As is standard procedure, such packages have instructions on them stating "Upon arrival please contact the addressee at the phone number listed below." I call the customer right away, waking them up, and inform them that their package of live baby chicks have just arrived here to the post office and are ready for pick up. The customer answers the phone on the fourth ring and says, with a muddled voice.

"H-h-hello," says the gentleman on the other end, clearing his throat.

"Good morning sir, sorry to bother you so early. This is Mr. V from the Creeks Bend Post Office calling to let you know that your shipment of baby chicks has just arrived and is now ready for pick up."

The gentleman then said, "Oh, ok thank you, I will be there in about an hour to pick them up. Where do I go once I arrive at your office?"

"Just come into the main lobby like you're going to purchase stamps and you will see a gray door directly in front of you. Next to that door you will see a doorbell, just push the button and someone will come and assist you."

"Ok great," replies the gentleman, "I will see you in a bit." and hangs up.

There are times when some of the chicks are not peeping at all.Uh oh! Perhaps some are sleeping. Yeah, that's it, you know, they have had a long journey and I'm certain there are some that are just plain tired, just sleepy…right? Yeah, right…I don't think so.

0530: The second transportation truck arrives from the plant with more letters, flats, parcels and several APC uprights of automated carrier routed flats, magazines, and large envelopes. So I begin helping the clerks to unload the truck.

Bitsy says to me, "Hey Mr. V, it's a good thing that Pudgy isn't here today or else she would file a grievance against you because you are helping unload the truck."

Pudgy used to be the alternate shop steward and as such would file a grievance at the drop of a hat whenever I would help to unload the truck stating that in doing so I was performing craft work and taking their jobs and potential overtime away. She was the only one who would complain about my helping unload trucks. The other employees welcomed my help especially when it was cold out.

Also at five thirty, Chip's smartphone goes off, just like clockwork, sounding the instrumental version of "We've Only Just Begun." It was one of Chip's and his late wife Chrisy's, favorite songs, as it embodied their hopes and dreams. It's Carly, Chip's daughter calling him as was her usual custom ever since her mother's passing. Carly had made a vow to her father that she would call him every morning during the work week, just so each could hear one another's voice before the start of the day. Chip used to call Chrisy every day upon the completion of his route. - On seeing his daughter's name and number appear- on the caller ID he answers it .

"Good morning honey," answers Chip with his still awakening, groggy voice.

"Good morning dad," replies Carly in an equal tone of voice. "It's Wednesday, rise and shine time…"it's time to make the donuts." After today you have only two more days left at work!"

"Yeah, I know."

"Are you anxious about retiring?" she asked.

"Oh, I'm a little apprehensive but I know its time for me to hang up the routine and those shoes and do something new."

"Yeah, you got a whole new life ahead of you young man…just follow the sun!" said Carly

Chip laughed and replied, "Now who's teaching who?"

"Well, I learned from the best." responded Carly.

"Yes, I can see." Chip answered.

"Anyhow dad, you have a great day. I'm going to try to catch another hour of sleep. Oh, and dad, are we still on for dinner this evening…seven o'clock right?"

"Yup, you got it, seven o'clock p.m. tonight! Just meet me there."

"Okay, dad I will."

"I love you, Carly, you have a great day and I will call you later after I finish my route."

"That's my dad, like clockwork! So long."

"So long, honey."

0535: Back at the supervisor desk, I notate the amount of mail that came in on the truck, and then proceed to correct clock ring errors in TAAS made from the employee's previous day's clock rings. This takes approximately thirty minutes depending on the amount of errors. In reality, it's the employee's responsibility, not management's, to input proper and accurate clock ring entries. Everyone gets a paycheck for doing their assigned work. During this time I also respond to emails sent from postal customers regarding complaints and various mail issues (example; missed delivered mail or missing packages). I will also retrieve customer's electronically generated hold mail and vacation notices. There are also emails from upper management that require prompt responses. Sometimes it just may be upper management sending informational tidbits indicating conference calls taking place later on.

0555: An employee by the name of Mason, the custodian, who happens to be hearing impaired, arrives to work and begins his daily walk around the office like he owns the place. After his "inspection" he will then stop and just stand in the middle of the workroom floor, with his hands in his pocket, and annoyingly stare at you. Don't look him in the eye or he will give you an earful, in his own way of communicating, which basically consists of grunts and the flailing of his arms.

Mason is also a tattle tale and will keep his eye on you if he suspects something. He will also tell you that such and such a person is "l-a-a-a-z-y." Besides being the custodian, and the town crier, Mason will perform minor maintenance and repairs on the postal vehicles. It seems as if he can fix most anything. He usually gets my attention by grunting "eh eh."

I'm sitting at the supervisor desk, with my eyes intently focused on the computer screen trying to ignore him. I do that whenever I see Mason approaching me because I know he's got something to complain about. I pretend as though I don't see him. As Mason nears me, he starts his frustrated grunting to get my attention.

"Eh Eh!"

However, I act as though he trying to get someone else's attention. But he keeps persisting in getting mine.

"Eh Eh!"

Defeated, I finally look up at him, with somewhat of a frown on my face, and I say "WHAT?" He then points to outside in the direction of the carrier loading dock.

"Traaays…traaays…ouuutside" he said in his way of talking. I then pointed to, and tapped my watch, and said to him "It's not six o'clock yet. You're not on the clock. Go away!" However, he kept on with his distressed groans. Eventually he stopped and walked away due to my ignoring him. I know that's not nice but he can be such a pain in the butt.

As he walked away, with CeeDee looking at us and grinning, he gestured to her. He motioned "No good no good." CeeDee just looked at me and laughed. But he kept on grumbling and saying "No good no good, l-a-a-azy l-a-a-a-zy, yeah"! Of course, he was referring to and pointing at me, not CeeDee.

0600: Mason clocks in at the time clock and as he places his time card back in the time card rack he turns to Bitsy and starts "Ouuutside ouuutside, messy messy." Samantha and Bitsy responded to him saying "Don't tell us, Mason, tell Mr. V, let Mr. V know." His reply to them, as he waved his index finger, was "la-zy, l-a-a-a-zy…yeah." Both Samantha and Bitsy laughed and Mason walked away and went outside to clean up the mess left behind by the carriers from the day before.

Everyone is busy at work. Now there are other chatter boxes, like this gal named Spice. We call her Spice simply because of her, well, spicy personality and the spicy foods she cooks. She's a woman of Thai descent and lives with her significant other. When I see Spice I will often mimic her by literally blurting out "blah blah blah blah blah blah blah" because of her Thai accent and her fast way of talking. Her usual response, whenever I mimic her, is "Oh, shut up." It's my little way of teasing her as she also likes to dish it out on me at times.

Spice loves to talk about and make fun of people. She also loves to spread gossip as do most of the employees. It seems that most of the employees are a bit "two-faced." They will smile to one another face to face and then become backstabbers by gossiping or ratting one another out.

Despite Spice's constant chatter, you can usually get a day's work out of her. When she's mad at you, you may get more. Spice's basic assignment is the retail window being the sales clerk in the post office, but sometimes I will bring her in early to assist with the distribution of mail before the carriers arrive. She works out at home on a daily basis, so she can handle the grunt work. It's postal policy to have eighty percent of the mail already spread around to the carrier cases prior to the carriers reporting for duty. This serves to keep them busy, working steadily. "Eight hours work for eight hours pay."

Spice is involved in what some might characterize as a strange relationship. She lives with a truck driver, who works for, you know, that other delivery company that begins with a U. When you have the combination of her mouth, mixed with his alcohol consumption there is bound to be a problem. It's like TNT! Together they have two little children, one boy, and one girl.

0635: The Postmaster, Meghyn, arrives to work. She dresses as if she works for some modeling agency of sort. This day, she has on this leopard print dress. Tight and clingy…certainly revealing, it's really not appropriate for wearing in such an environment as the post office. But Meghyn wears what she wants, and pretty much does what she wants. She also has on a pair of what looks like four-inch high heel shoes to complement her outfit. I think she enjoys the added height that comes from the high heels. She would prefer you looking up at her as opposed to her looking up at you. I believe that's why she wears such high heels, but I must admit her shoes are very stylish.

A mixed blonde, she's about 49 years old and is a high energy person. Approximately five feet eight inches tall in bare feet, she's darn near close to six foot depending on the height of high heels she wearing. She has presence and you better believe she knows it. She is very attractive, a head turner for sure. But I think she wears a bit too much make-up. She's a busty woman and she definitely does not try hard to hide it. She impresses me as having a healthy sized ego… she knows she's got the goods if you catch my drift. She is very proud of and most confident in her appearance as can be seen by the clothes she wears.

Meghyn is the energy of the office. She can start a fire and she can also put it out! However, most times she will start a fire and then leave it up to me to put it out. Her style of management is the shotgun approach, bullets flying everywhere. If she has a beef with someone you had better duck. She can be like a pit bull and when she locks on to a problem employee, removing that person from the post office rolls is her goal. She has a very good track record.

She is very good at drilling you for information and getting to the root of the problem. Trust me I have seen her in action. In fact, to be honest, I have been on the receiving end of her relentless drilling. Now don't get me wrong, despite the anxiety she gives me, in many ways I admire her. I find her to be intelligent, knowledgeable, and very courageous.

When she walks in the first thing you hear is the entrance door creaking as it slowly closes behind her. The sound of her high heels clicking on the floor like taps then follows. Next, you hear her postmaster's office door keys jingling in her hands. She opens the door, walks into it and closes the door behind her and will remain in the office for say, five to ten minutes. One of the clerks, usually Pudgy, realizing that Meghyn has arrived, will say "Okay Mr. V, let the games begin!"

It's at this time that I will get up from the supervisor desk and will walk to the men's room. I will stay in there for a few minutes.

Actually, more like several minutes until the shock of her arrival wears off and I gain my nerves. Honestly, I just have this problem with Meghyn walking out onto the workroom floor and the first thing she sees is me sitting on my butt at the supervisor's station desk, even though I'm working and performing part of my day to day, week to week, daily routines. I just feel uncomfortable having her see me sitting there. I suppose it goes back to when I was the second shift supervisor and basically oversaw the carrier side of the operation only. Such job required that I walk around the floor and or stand up and constantly observe the carriers, like some security guard.

Actually, I did less work then than I do now. The former supervisor whose job was abolished, because he was the "low the man on the totem pole" and headquarters insisted that our office did not require the additional supervisor hours needed to manage the floor, would download the reports off the computer and supervise the morning distribution clerk operation. His roll permitted me to report to work later in the morning and devote full attention observing the employees, mostly the mail carriers, both in the office and on the street as they delivered the mail.

After several minutes of getting my nerves together, I walk out of the men's room and back to my supervisor station and proceed with what I had been doing. This routine of me going to the men's room is something I did virtually every day when Meghyn arrived. On Saturday's when she's off I don't do it. The atmosphere is definitely different when she's around.

0645: Meghyn, as she comes out of her office with her upbeat walk and a smile that could light up Manhattan, starts with her typical greeting…"Good morning CeeDee.Good morning Samantha." "Hi Meghyn." they both respond. She continues on, "Good morning Bitsy." "Good morning Meghyn."

"Hey, where's Mr. V? He's never at his desk when I come out…you ever notice that?" she asks.

"I think he went into the men's room." responds Bitsy.

"Hmmm, my presence must make him have to pee pee," said Meghyn.

"Yeah, it seems you have that effect on him! Besides Meghyn, if I were Mr. V, I would run into the restroom too if I heard the clicks of your heels coming." They all chuckle.

As Meghyn takes a walk into the ladies room herself, I emerge from the men's room and return to the supervisor desk.

"Hey, Mr. V did you pee pee out your stress?" asked Samantha.

"Hahaha, very funny Samantha." I replied.

Eventually, Meghyn comes out of the ladies room, sees me at the supervisor desk, walks over and greets me.

"Good morning V!"

My usual internal response is "What's good about it"...of course, I will say that under my breath. "Good Meghyn, how are you this morning?"

"Well, first let me take a walk around and inspect the situation and then I will let you know. Hey, V, what's up with the deal that when I walk out of my office you're never at the supervisor desk? You're always in the men's room. What's the matter, can't you hold your water?" She asked with a smile not really expecting an answer.

"Actually Meghyn your arrival in the morning makes me do the double P."

"The double P, what's that?"

"Pee and Pray," I responded.

"Hahahahaha, pee and pray? Do I have that much effect on you V?"

"Yup, you are hard on a man, Meghyn."

"Oh, come on now! Now you're starting to sound like Mario."

"Well, Meghyn, I responded, the bible does say that *"men everywhere should always pray."* Even in the men's room."

"Oh, really? And what bible version is it that says pee and pray... the New King James?"

"Nooo."

"Oh, I get it…wait don't tell me…it's the Newly Revised New King James version?"

"Hahaha…wow, Meghyn…now you're on your way to becoming a biblical scholar!"

"Yeah, those Sunday school days are finally starting to pay off," was her reply.

Well, following that discourse, Meghyn marches off and takes a quick walk around to inspect the condition and status of the mail processing. She'll ask if the transportation trucks have been on time and how much mail arrived on each truck, and you better have an answer. Then she will start barking out orders. Everyone says yes to Meghyn. **Nobody ever says no to her.** We may hesitate or give useless reasons why something can't be done. Ultimately, we obey her instructions. "Whatever Lola wants, Lola gets." Her boyfriend refers to her as the "Queen Bee" and brother she can pack a sting.

Meghyn is very competitive and can be an "in your face" type of manager. She has no problem with being confrontational. She once told me there was a time when she had thought of becoming a police officer. Trust me I had no problem in believing that! At one moment she can tell you I'm going to fire you and then the next moment she will be laughing with you and asking how your family. All in all, believe it or not, I really don't mind working with her, despite the many times it felt like acid was eating away at the inside of my stomach. I suppose being able to look at such an attractive woman every day such as Meghyn helps to make the aggravation worthwhile. Hey, what can I say, she's got it going on!

Well, Mr. "Tattle Tale" Mason, returned back in from outside as Meghyn was walking around and quickly went up to her and started complaining to her about the mess the carriers had left from the previous day and how he had to clean it all up.

Meghyn then responded by saying "Huh, what, where"?

"Ooooutside, messy, ooooutside!"

"Huh…again?" said Meghyn.

He motioned at her with his index finger as if to say, "Come with me."

Both went outside and he explained to her, in his own signature way, what the carrier dock had looked like before his cleaning it all up. But she just shook her head and came back inside. As a result, she approached me and said, "That Mason, he's such a tattle tale. However, I want you to have a conversation with the carriers about properly storing empty mail trays and mail bins." Then she said to me, with her hand on her hip, "Everyday out there should be looking as good as I look…shouldn't it V?" Then she flashed that wide smile at me, as she turned and walked away like a runway model.

Note: One thing that I have noticed is that when Meghyn gives an order or instruction the employees say "yes" or "okay." But let me give the same order or instruction and I encounter opposition, complaining and negativity. I have come to believe that postal employees, though they complain about tough managers, give the tough managers more respect than the easy going and caring type. The nice, kind and caring supervisors and managers get taken advantage of.

0650: The first few mailmen, or should I say, mail carriers, began arriving to work. (As more women joined the work force and started delivering mail, the term mail carrier emerged.) A few mail carriers habitually report to work thirty to forty-five minutes early and go to the swing room aka lunch room. They will read their newspaper, drink their morning coffee or juice and chill out before the *games* begin. Of course, there are those employees who habitually report to work five to ten minutes late every day, and even some as much as fifteen to twenty minutes late. Ultimately, I will give such employees what's known as an 'Official Discussion'. If they continue to be late then the next step is to issue an Official Disciplinary letter. Such discipline could, but rarely does, escalate up to and removal from the post office. I think that's one of the problems with the postal system; there's not much accountability at the employee craft level, but only at the front line management levels. So there's virtually no fear of losing one's job. The presence of strong unions may have something to do with it as well, especially the mail carriers union which is the largest union in the post office.

Continuing on with Meghyn, upon her inspection of things, she returns to me and proceeds to ask me about the previous day's reports and go over the employee's performances as noted in the system known as DOS. However, this morning she quickly asks me "Did anybody call out today?"

"Yes," I reply.

"Who?"

"Monique."

"WHAT…Monique?! Call her back right now and tell her she will have to provide us with medical documentation from her doctor stating that she is incapacitated for duty."

"Well I was going to inform Monique of that when I tried calling her back."

"WHAT?!" exclaimed Meghyn, *"Tried* calling her back?"

"Yes! When she originally called out she caught me off guard because I was so disgusted and angry that I forgot to tell her. So I called her back to inform her that she will need to provide us medical documentation but I only got her answering machine."

"Ok, then I want you to go out to her house right now, knock on her door and tell her in person. Do you know where she lives V?"

"Not exactly," I said, "but I can look her address up in her personnel file and find her residence."

"What an idiot…can you believe that chick?! Yet she wants to get hired here and become a regular."

"Yeah, Meghyn, I know. I will get out to her place right away!"

"Hey, V, before you go, how did the carriers do yesterday? Do you have the reports ready? Where are they?" she asked.

"Yes, I do Meghyn, they're right here."

"Good, let me see them. Hmmm, Zakar is getting over on you V! Look at his numbers. Why was he in the office so long? Look at his street time. He overran his projections by forty-five minutes! What was he doing? What took him so long? You gotta take him in the office V! I want answers and I want action taken! Oh, my god! You know I'm gonna have to explain his times, once again, to my boss V! He's gonna want to know why we failed to make projections yesterday…and he's gonna want to know what are we gonna do to fix it! Action, alright V! I want, I need action!"

I nod my head 'yes' as I begin to feel that acid burning sensation in my stomach.

Turning on her heels, Meghyn yells back to me "Remember this V, to get what you want in life, you're going to have to be a pain in the butt. You're gonna have to get on somebody's last nerves."

"Yeah, well, you must be getting what you want Meghyn because you sure are getting on mine," I replied.

"Hey, watch that young man," she said, and then she flashed that familiar Meghyn wide grin. Wow, I thought to myself, what a Heckle Jyde personality she has. But I suppose this place and these people will make you like that.

Such questioning is one of worst parts of the day for me as it relates to how I feel about Meghyn and the post office. Such drilling will make any supervisor's stomach churn. Though she has become easier to work for. There was a time when she was even worse to work for so I hear; she can still get to you. It's usually during such questioning that she will share with me, when applicable, what the hot topic of the day is going to be as it relates to the post office and upper management. By hot topic I mean, what upper management is focusing on as far as productivity.

As we walk away from each other I just shake my head saying to myself *Man this place is a trip...what a job!* **As a front line supervisor, you catch hell from upper management as well as from the craft personnel. You are caught right in middle like a sandwich. From day one when I first started this job, I questioned whether it was the right decision. I'm not saying it was the wrong decision but it sure has been hellish. I thank God for his strength.**

Note: The Letter Carrier union does not recognize the reports that are generated by the DOS system, especially when it may involve corrective or disciplinary action taken against one of their members. They primarily don't recognize it because the mail volume amount entered into DOS is based on a linear mail count and not a piece count. A piece count is more accurate than a linear count, but performing a piece would require much more counting time on management's part. Actually, I'm all for mail piece counts as it does provide a more accurate and reliable measurement.

Having witnessed the exchange with Meghyn, Samantha walks up to me and quietly whispers, "I don't know how you put up with her Mr. V…better you than me. I think I would quit or even go back to the employee craft position if I were in your shoes."

"Well, just remember I said this to you Samantha; one day I'm gonna cast this job aside like a dirty garment, leave and never look back."

"Oh, hahaha, ok Mr. V, I won't forget." she replied as she laughed, as though she didn't believe me. The attitude around here is nobody leaves the post office, you just die.

0655: I proceed to go out to Monique's house. Meghyn instructed Samantha to clock onto operation "higher level" to start downloading the rest of the DOS reports. Higher Level pay is used when a non-managerial person is instructed by their superior to perform managerial duties. Usually, Samantha won't mind…hey it pays a little more money. Meghyn also had Samantha count, record, and enter mail the volumes into the DOS system while I was out of the office so that, when I returned, I could obtain an estimated workload for each carrier assigned to their various route. For example, if a carrier or route has approximately two feet of letters or magazines, the time taken to sort such mail into each individual address slot should take about twenty to thirty minutes or basically fifteen minutes for each one foot of mail, depending on the thickness of the mail. So, in theory, a mail carrier is expected to case four feet of mail within an hours times...give or take a few, again, depending on the thickness of the mail pieces, like thin pieces versus thick pieces. Three inches of thick sized mail will not take nearly as long to case as three inches of thin sized mail such as political mail flyers. You may have only five or six pieces of thick mail within two inches, while on the other hand if it's really thin mail then you could possibly have three hundred pieces. Catch my drift?

Typically during this time I will pivot or split up routes which I partition out on a piece of paper. Such routes called open or vacant routes, will not have a carrier assigned to them on that given day. Therefore, a carrier will deliver his or her own route as well as a portion of that vacant route. Depending on the amount of time as well as mail volumes such sections of an open route are delivered on under time hours or what is called a pivot. A pivot means the carrier does not have eight hours worth of work on their own route for the day so they will be expected to carry a segment of another route so as to give that employee a fair eight hours of work. However, most mail carrier employees do not buy into the pivoting idea. They do not like being told that they have under time or pivoting time. They want that time to be considered over time.

0700: The last transportation truck arrives with our automated letter. These letters are in plastic trays and are placed onto metal racks until the carriers are ready to leave for the street. The carriers do not have to case these letters into their cases as these letters are already in delivery order. Meghyn orders one of the clerks to stage the trays of letters on the racks.

0715: Katie, a White woman, was born and raised in South Philadelphia, shows up for work. Her reporting time is 0700 hours but because of the distance she has to travel (little more than an hour) and traffic she is usually late. I've given her several discussions and have written her up. Then for a period of time she will show up for work on time, until the disciplinary action is expunged from her file, and then it's back to being late again. Nevertheless, I put Katie on what is known as breakdown and the spreading of carrier routed tubs and trays of letters. Later on in the morning I instruct Katie to assist with the scanning of parcels. All effort is geared towards getting the mail to carriers as early as possible so that they, the carriers, can get out onto the street and deliver the mail. Customers, particularly business customers, want their mail early, not late. That's one of the reasons the post office has pushed automation. Automation has enabled the post office to process mail in a more accurate and efficient manner.

The first flow of customers begins to arrive at eight-thirty A.M; when the retail window opens. At about eight fifteen, Katie will begin the process of getting the retail area ready for business. This means stocking the cash drawer, stocking and properly displaying stamps to be sold, and turn on the retail machines for the daily transactions that will take place. The retail window will remain operating until it closes at five o'clock P.M. The retail window does not close down for lunch break, but each retail clerk will be given a lunch hour, sometimes thirty minutes when necessary, which is covered by other retail clerks.

Katie used to work at a large mail processing plant in another district or region. I've overheard her saying how they, she and other employees, would clock in at the plant and then go back out to their car and catch a nap, especially if they were on the first shift, which is the graveyard shift. Apparently, the managers couldn't keep track of all the employees because the plant was so large, and some managers just didn't care. However, because of declining mail volumes and thus declining revenues, due to the internet and sluggish economy, she was one of many employees who were either forced to relocate, cross over to another craft or simply take early retirement. Katie chose to relocate.

Katie reminds me of Joan Rivers, you know? She has that "Can we talk?" like persona, and comes across as being somewhat of an air head. However I don't think she is. Of course, Joan Rivers was no air head either. Katie, a divorcee, is now on her second marriage and apparently this one is not going well either.

When it comes to the distribution side of her job Katie needs focus. Of course, then there's the typical complaint of some physical ailment. You know like, back, neck or some type of tendonitis which then either slows her down or even prohibits her, like so many other employees, from performing their basic daily tasks. However, on the other hand, she is a pretty good retail window clerk because of her friendly nature and the fact she ***loves*** to talk. I think Katie needs to be around people. Some employees don't like working with the public or postal customers as they would rather perform manual labor type activities without dealing with customers. Katie, however, is really a social butterfly, and doesn't mind when she is assigned to the retail window operation.

Katie and I often reminisce about the old cartoons and comedy shows, especially the "Three Stooges." We can often be heard getting one another's attention by shouting "Hey, Moe" whenever we see each other approaching or needed the other person's attention. Then we might pause for a moment and have a conversation within a particular character role or show. The humor helped us to deal with the repetitive stress of the job. That's basically Katie's deal.

0720: I arrive back to the office after taking the trip out to Monique's house. It was a wasted trip as Monique did not answer the door. But you know as I think about it, it really wasn't a wasted trip because upper management loves to hear that a supervisor would go to such an extent as to drive out to an employee's house. It's like they love it when you harass an employee, though they won't admit it. They also say it sends a message to the other employees.

Noticing that I have returned, Meghyn approaches me and inquires as to how the trip out to Monique's house went. I informed her that Monique never answered the door so I was unable to speak with her.

"Yeah, right sick," said Meghyn. "She probably wasn't home. She's probably spent the night at her boyfriends house." She continued, "Make sure you give her a welcome back to work discussion when she reports for work tomorrow. And make sure you document it. In fact, pull up her attendance record for me. I want to know what her attendance has been like for the past ninety days. I'm sick and tired of these people calling out sick. Heck V, you and I don't always feel like coming to work but we do! Why should it be any different for them?"

"Yeah, Meghyn I know," I responded.

"Personally, I think the Post Office gives out far too much sick leave. Where else can you find a job that will give you up to four weeks of sick leave every year and then let you carry over into the next year whatever balance of the sick leave you don't use? You know what the problem is V?

I looked at her as if to ask, " No, what?"

"Entitlement! Employees today have this sense of entitlement." she said with her hands flailing in the air. "They're just like children. They're worse than children…entitlement! Well, they need to know that management has entitlements too, and we're entitled to take corrective action against them. How about that for entitlement, V?"

She then looked at me and smiled and then said, "I'm sorry V, I know you're not the one who called out. I guess I had to get that off my chest. And don't you even go there V, I know what you're thinking when I referred to my chest!"

And with that she smiled, turned about, and walked away with her heels clicking in rhythm.

You know what? I hate to admit it but that's exactly what I was thinking.

Bitsy, who was standing and witnessed the conversation, said to me, as Meghyn walked away out of sight, "I sure am glad I don't have your job Mr. V…you couldn't pay me enough to sit in your seat."

I just walked away and murmured, "Yeah right, they don't pay me enough,"

0725: Most of the mail carriers have now arrived to work and begin forming a line at the time clock waiting to clock in. There are all kinds of conversations going at this time even some jockeying for position to clock in first.

0730 - 0733: The mail carriers clock into work and immediately proceed outside to do the daily inspection of their mail trucks to see if there may be any operational issues with their respective vehicles. Such vehicle inspections are a mandatory part of the mail carriers job. If there are issues with a truck it must be corrected prior to the vehicle being taken onto the street. For instance, there may be a problem with the turn signals or with the horn, tires, or even the brakes. Whatever the issue it must be corrected before the vehicle is allowed to be driven. SAFETY FIRST is the motto!

One of the carriers is an employee by the name Buster. Occasionally I will call him "OT" short for "Old Timer" because though only in his mid-forties he acts like an old grumpy man. His job position is carrier route number fourteen. Buster often calls me "Witness" because I once wrote a statement for another supervisor when I observed Buster getting belligerent and being insubordinate with the other supervisor. I saw Buster aggressively getting in the supervisor's face taunting him and thus causing a hostile environment. Due to the statement I wrote, Buster was put on a 'Two Year Good Conduct, or else Removal from Post Office Discipline.'

That being said, Buster walks through the doors and loudly says…

"Drop your drawls…I'm out" and then starts chuckling as he obnoxiously butts into the line, grabs his timecard and clocks in. Buster is a 6'2" Black man weighing a solid two hundred fifty pounds and likes to intimidate management and others with his husky tone. If you say, "Good morning Buster," his usual reply will be "What's so damn good about it, huh?" In the past, he has been known to threaten management by saying "You just keep messing with me and I'm gonna get my gun." Despite his several threats, he's still working for the post office. Needless to say, the post office would be better off without the likes of him. Oddly enough there are a few employees who like Buster, or they appear at least to like him. Maybe it's just their way of putting up with him. Most managers hate him. However, I have to admit, there are times when he can really make you laugh. I mean this guy can really bust your sides laughing and he knows it. I think he uses that to his advantage.

Anyway, the other employees standing in line just let him be and choose not to oppose him. Why bother, it's useless anyway.

Another carrier whose name is Willie, is on carrier route number thirteen, and has been in the postal service for nearly thirty-seven years. He also served in the U. S. Army for two years. Simply put, everybody likes Willie, that is, everybody but the postmaster. She does not trust him one bit. Quite frankly, I don't blame her. Willie always seems to be working his game. Nevertheless, he and I somehow get along. It helps you to like people when you can see beyond their faults, or at least see beyond how they act at work while on the clock.

Willie is the union's local representative for the carrier craft in our office. As a shop steward, Willie is a little sneaky at times. It pays for management to know the language of the various contracts the post office has with the respective unions and any postal manuals regarding policies and procedures. Basically, Willie is a nice guy and very well liked by his peers, as well as the community he serves.

I remember the first day I met Willie he strolled up to me with his chest sticking out and said; "Mr. V, you may be the supervisor but just remember this one thing I run things around here and as long as you remember that, you'll be okay." Then he chuckled.

Willie LOVES the women, or as he says "All the women love me." One of his favorite expressions is "Honey, don't call me when you need me, call me when you want me!" Then he'll bend over chuckling and cracking himself up. Despite the fact that he has been employed by the postal service for so long a time, he is virtually penniless. He picks up money on the side by refereeing. Willie has made some bad business decisions during his lifetime. I doubt if he ever files his taxes on time. I hear he owes everyone and the man on the moon. Yet he simply has an 'I'm going to enjoy life' attitude. Willie, when he talks, sounds just like the late comedian Jimmy Durante.

In walks Willie, and as usual, he says…"Well, once again, here I am world! God's gift to the world!" before chuckling away. The people shake their heads, especially Old Man.

Old Man, a White man, is carrier route number ten, and has been employed in the Post Office for forty-two years and has served in the U.S. Army as well. He actually trained Willie on Willie's first day in the post office. What a story that was. Old Man, sometimes called "Pop," is seventy-five years old, and has the, I guess I should say, privilege of being the oldest carrier in our district.

Old Man suffers from a severe case of Rheumatoid Arthritis as well as high blood pressure. The pain is so unbearable at times yet he persists on not retiring. Due to his age and physical maladies Old Man moves around pretty slowly. Yet we can't force him to retire. Old Man has maxed out his years when it comes to his pension percentage as he is at the highest percentage that can he earn in the Post Office. I have asked Old Man "Why don't you retire?" His usual response is; "Well Mr. V quite honestly I'm scared to retire. You see," he continues, "when my father retired he died six months later. I know it sounds stupid and everyone, including my wife, tells me that that was his life and not mine, but for that reason, I've been scared to take that step. I'm literally afraid to retire," he says as his body and hands tremble. He then chuckles a bit and proceeds to say to me "Heck Mr. V, I will probably die in this place and you can have my body. And it's not just because of my father's death but gosh the same thing has happened to two of my closest friends. Both my father's passing and the death of those guys haunts me to this day. Besides, "he continues, with head and hands tremoring, "I don't know…I mean what would I do with my time? Being a mailman is all I've ever done…it's all I know."

Then there's the carrier on route number eleven, named Reds. Reds, a White man, stands about 6' 4" tall, big boned, and very slim. His movements are somewhat robotic mostly due to health conditions and medication that he takes for his anxiety. He likes to ask technical questions such as "How much is the load bearing weight of the roof"? He is by far the most miserable and angriest employee in the office. I think he's been angry since birth just mad at the world for being born. A college graduate with a degree in Civil Engineering, Reds, from what I hear, resents being in the post office. Apparently, he didn't have the temperament and proper conduct for traditional corporate America. Reds likes to argue and is usually a disagreeable type individual. A bitter person, he has a chip on his shoulders and does not like being told what to do. Now, if it is his idea then he goes for it. One of his favorite sayings is, "I can be your best friend or your worst enemy." Reds is known for being able to dish it out but on the other hand, he can't take it.

On route number twelve, there's a carrier by the name of Lynn a White woman with sandy blonde hair, fairly tall, rather busty and curvy. If Postmaster Meghyn is the Queen of the post office then Lynn is the Princess. Lynn, a forty-year-old divorcee, is known for her sexual escapades. Prior to my coming to this office, Lynn, as the story goes, was rumored to have made out with the previous postmaster, married of course, while on the clock, in the postmaster's office. They were never fired because no one ever eyeballed it nor could they obtain a statement from anyone who knew her story. The only reason it's known is because she supposedly shared the story with a few other postal friends. Lynn yaks all the time. It's like she can't control herself. Personally, I think she consumes way too much caffeine!

She usually wears skorts, and can often be heard saying, when she bends over, "Hey Mr. V, so and so is looking at me." She's a real tease and knows it. She likes the attention and she plays the role really well. Of course, all of the guys love Lynn. I used to like her until I got to know her. That was when I became a supervisor and had to deal with her on a different level. She is a crafty devil with blonde hair and green eyes.

I get the feeling that there is a bit of a looks competition between the Queen and the Princess even though Meghyn has nearly ten years on Lynn.

Then there are these two carriers, Marlon and Zakar whose cases are right behind the supervisor desk. These two employees remind me of the characters in the movie titled *Dumb & Dumber.* You have to see and hear them to really appreciate what I mean. These two are a real comedy show, and quite honestly they're not as dumb as they appear, it's just the way they come across. They are a show indeed.

Marlon is a very hard worker and is on carrier route number nine. He's a really good employee and is very accommodating to management, or at least he is to me when the need calls for it. He rarely calls out sick which is a real plus. Actually, I don't recall the last time he had called out sick. I'd have to check his attendance record in the timekeeping system to find out.

So let me describe Marlon to you. If Willie is God's gift to the world, then Marlon will tell you that he is God's gift to women. Though he is married Marlon gives the impression that he is a player. However, from what I hear, he's one of the few around here who happens to have a successful marriage. Personally, I think he is all talk because I never heard of him ever having any extra-marital affairs, or at least ever getting caught. Marlon likes wearing his postal shirt half buttoned to show the black hair on his chest. He thinks it's sexy. The black hair on his head is slicked back with lots of gel in it.

Marlon has lots of energy. He loves to play golf and therefore plays in a golf league after work during the golf season. I hear he's not that good though. He's a high handicap golfer, struggles to break ninety-five for eighteen holes of golf. But he loves to have fun and be out with the guys. He's my go-to guy when I'm in a real crunch. Marlon loves the overtime money.

Then there's Zakar, whom Marlon often refers to as "Bones" because of his tall slender build, is an East African-born, non-practicing Muslim and is carrier on route number eight. Zakar is a hand full, to say the least. Zakar, it seems, is always up to no good. Although Zakar comes across as this nice, innocent person he really is a sneaky individual who can not be trusted to follow instructions. I heard from a previous supervisor of his where he worked prior to our office that he often would enter false clock rings so as to get paid more than he was entitled to. However, that supervisor for one reason or another never did anything to him but would only give him warnings or official discussions. So Zakar, as the saying goes, slipped through the cracks during his probationary period and was permanently hired.

If you give him orders for the day he will say "Sure, okay, no problem." and then will go about it in his way, which is usually contrary to what you tell him. Zakar always has excuses and it's always someone else's fault when he fails to follow instructions.

Zakar always talks about how he prefers big women. He will tell you "I like them with big panties." He and I have known each other for about twelve years as we were co-employees at another post office. I did attempt to terminate him a couple of times but the decisions were always overturned by Human Resources because of a technicality in his employment status. Actually, the postmaster, Meghyn, was a bit too impulsive in directing me to issue him a "Letter of Removal," which I did and thus he was technically removed from the postal rolls. However, due to the fact that he had already completed his initial ninety day probation period as a new employee, Zakar awarded his job back,with lost pay no doubt. The ruling which worked in his favor essentially stated that an employee can only serve one probationary period. It was basically the same as the "double jeopardy" rule. You know, Zakar appropriately could have been nicknamed Nine Lives.

All morning long Marlon and Zakar go back and forth at each other calling each other names and downplaying each one's ability to do the job. I really think they like each other but have more fun poking at one another. I see their comedy show as a stress reliever for them as it helps them to get through the daily morning ritual of casing mail. When Marlon gets in a good shot at him, Zakar will say "Oh, good one." Hey, it's part of the everyday conversations that goes on in this place.

I've given routes ten through thirteen a nickname which I refer to as "Amen Corner" just like the golf holes at the annual Master's golf tournament which is probably one of professional golf's most celebrated events of the year. The reason I refer to it as Amen Corner is because once I've made it past those characters I will then say to myself "Amen" as though I have ended a prayer. The carriers love it.

Then there is the employee named Gino. Gino, another divorcee, who was awarded custody of his son, is a "Rural Carrier" and acts as the Rural Carrier union representative. Rural Carriers deliver mail to the outskirts part of town, in the rural areas, hence the term. They're also on a different pay system. City Carriers, Clerks, and Mail Handlers are paid by an hourly rate. Rural Carriers get paid by an evaluated route rate or system. In other words, their routes are given a particular dollar value and hour value which is basically based on the number of mail stops, the volume of mail, mileage, and daily number average of packages. However, if a rural carrier can do his or her route in less than the evaluated time they will still receive the full evaluated pay. Now the flip side of the coin is that if it takes the rural carrier longer than the evaluated rate then they will only receive the evaluated rate pay. So it behooves them to work faster, and Gino works fast. He has it down to a science.

Gino, rural carrier number one, is also the safety committee chair here at the office. Most of the employees dislike Gino especially Reds. Oh, how Reds hates him. An individual who loves to brag Gino can often be heard boasting about how fast he is and how good of an employee he is and how well he treats his customers. He has also, on numerous occasions, bragged about how high he scored on the supervisor's entry level test. However, to this day he has never stepped into management.

Gino, a college grad with TWO degrees, an accomplishment he loves to talk about, is a well read and very informed current events type individual. He really loves to talk about politics and the stock market. Apparently, when he leaves work he will go straight home, get online, and play the stock market. I would have to describe Gino as having an ADHDlike personality.

I must admit that Gino is an excellent carrier when it comes to speed, proficiency, and productivity, and he is very conscientious about his job performance and customer satisfaction. Always operating at a high pace, he sometimes appears to work unsafe. However, he has never been involved in a postal industrial or motor vehicle accident, at least not while being under my watch.

Having a rough on the edges appearance, he has the look of one of those ultimate fighter guys and comes across, at least initially, as being inpatient and real tough. Despite being a union representative, he typically does not like conflicts.

The next individual that I will introduce is an employee who goes by the name of Oliver. Oliver, another divorcee, is the carrier on route number seven. Oliver is a scruffy looking, short and stubby middle age man who sports a Mohawk haircut from time to time, and wears earrings. I know it's not nice to say, and I have been told such, and

I'm sure you've heard the expression, but Oliver looks like a person who climbed out from under a rock. He periodically suffers from a bad and painful case of Shingles. Admittedly, he also suffers from depression and lots of it. However, Oliver rarely misses work. He is believed to be gay but has never admitted to it nor has anyone ever seen him in a homosexual relationship, however, the employees tease him about it constantly. He doesn't seem to mind the teasing. I think it's safe to say he's bi-sexual. Admitting to being either homosexual or even bisexual, in this post office, for him would be like committing suicide. The employees, the way they feel about him, would eat him alive.

Now Oliver is not the most popular of employees and is probably the least liked. Simply put, Oliver is a supervisor's headache. His work performance is poor and he requires a lot of supervision. But he's not only a supervisor's headache due to his work performance, but also because of the other employees. The other employees see his lack of performance and are quick to let management know about it. You know how tattle tales are. They don't mind holding management, and other employees accountable, just don't hold them accountable.

Trust me when I say that numerous attempts have been made at firing Oliver and yet each attempt has failed. Maybe one day he will just up and quit because he's really not cut out for this type of work or environment? Despite my feelings about Oliver, I do believe the various medications he takes for his ailments adversely affect his ability to focus and perform as a mail carrier. Whatever can go wrong with Oliver will go wrong. He is a problem waiting to happen. Man, I tell ya, there are some real characters in the postal office and he's one of them. You may have to dig a little but in all honesty, he does have a nice side to him…he can be polite.

Then there is Rico, they call him Rico because he is from Puerto Rico. Rico is a hard working man and a dedicated Christian. He habitually arrives to work forty-five to fifty minutes early every day and goes straight into the lunch room and eats his breakfast. Then once finished eating he will proceed to his case and read his bible.

Rico is a good person but can at times get on my nerves because of his mumbling and complaining attitude.

In the post office, Rico is known as a "Utility Carrier or Sub" because he cases and carries five different routes per week. This simply means that he will carry a particular route when the regular carrier is scheduled off that day. In other, words five out of the six days Rico will carry a different route every day, and is off, on his sixth days. So all carriers and clerks operate on a five-day weekly work schedule and are off one day a week as well as Sunday. This is due to the post office currently delivering mail six days a week Monday thru Saturday. However, there have been a few attempts to overturn the mandate that was originally enacted by congress years ago and cut mail delivery to five days. If that were to happen, job positions such as the one Rico has would be abolished. Whether that is good or bad for the overall financial health of the Post office, you can believe the mail carriers union has consistently fought such a move.

Just a note here, the mail processing plants generally operate seven days a week twenty-four hours a day.

The telephone rings. "Good morning Creeks Bend Post Office, Mr. V speaking can I help you?"

"Good morning and thanks for taking my call. I'm sorry but what did you say your name was again?" asked the woman on the other end.

"My name is Mr. V."

"Hmmm, Mr. V, is that an Asian name?"

"No ma'am it's not."

"Oh, okay. Well, how do you spell it?"

"It's just the letter V. It's an initial. It's short for Ventnor." I explained.

"Say that name again?"

"Ventnor."

"Betner?"

"No, Ventnor."

"Hmmm, spell it for me."

" V-E-N-T-N-O-R."

"Oh, Ventnor, like Ventnor Avenue on the old board game called Monopoly?"

"Yup, that's it!"

"Wow, that's an interesting name. Tell me, where did you get that name from?"

"I got it from my parents."

"Well, of course, you got it from your parents. But how did you get it, get the name Ventnor?"

"Well, as the story goes, names starting with the letter V ran in our family and so my parents were looking for something different, something other than Victor or Vincent. During my mother's pregnancy my family was driving through New Jersey on a vacation and my eldest brother saw a sign which read Ventnor, New Jersey. So he said to my parents, "Hey, let's name him Ventnor." Well, apparently they agreed and the name stuck."

"Oh, that's such a wonderful story. I love to hear names that have a story behind them. Much like the Native American Indians, stated the woman. Well, I'm sure that when you answered this phone call, you did not think you would have to explain the origin of your name to someone, did you?"

"No, I did not," I replied.

"Right, right…now let's see…oh my, I forgot why I called. Hmmm, why did I call? Gee whiz, that's so embarrassing. I don't remember why I called. Please forgive, but please, can you tell me your name? I'm so very sorry."

"Ma'am, my name is Mr. V."

"Mr. V?"

"Yes, my name is Mr. V."

"And please tell me, how do you spell that?"

Oh, my goodness, not again, this person must have dementia or Alzheimer's, I mumbled to myself.

"V…it's simply the letter V. It's short for Ventnor. V-E-N-T-N-O-R!"

"Oh, okay! Ventnor…what an interesting name…I like that. You know, it seems like I just heard that name recently."

"Yes, ma'am, I'm sure you have," I replied.

"Oh, you think so too huh?"

"Yes, ma'am, I know you did. Anyway, my name is Mr. V and this is the Creeks Bend Post Office, how can I help you today?"

"I thought you said your name was Ventnor."

"Yes, ma'am it is, but people call me Mr. V for short."

"Well, Mr. V I called you? Oh, dear, I don't remember why. Why did I call you? I'm so sorry sir. You must think I'm losing my mind. And I'm so sorry for calling you, sir. I know you have a name. Did I ask you your name?"

"Yes, ma'am. You did. But listen, how about if you hang up the phone, think about it and then perhaps you might remember why you called, and then you can call me back if you like."

"Oh, what a wonderful idea! You're such a nice man. What a gentleman you are. I'm going to make sure my husband knows what a wonderful person you are. And very interesting too! Well, goodbye and nice talking to you. We'll have to do this again soon, okay?"

"Yeah, right."

"Goodbye!"

"Goodbye, ma'am."

Then I looked at Katie, who was in earshot of the conversation, and said to her, "How about you answering some of these phone calls?"

"No way, but you hang in there Moe…and don't let them stress you out! Do you remember that commercial on TV that used to come on? It went something like this 'When you let them stress you out, you get sick. When you get sick, you call out from work. When you call out from work, you get fired. When you get fired, you got no money. And when you got no money, your wife leaves you. Don't let your wife leave you!'"

"Hahahahah…that was a good one Katie!" and we both chuckled.

I got up from the supervisor's desk and followed the carriers outside to the loading dock to watch them inspect their vehicles.

Buster, as he's walking to his postal vehicle starts singing, loud enough for me to hear, "It always feel like somebody's watching me."

Lynn chimes in on the song by saying "and I have no privacy."

Reds finishes it off by saying "Oh-oh-oh-oh."

"Yeah, yeah yeah very funny! Come on folks, just get your vehicles inspected, I responded, and let's get back inside and start casing up the mail."

"Oh, come on Mr. V, can't we have a little fun around here. I guess Mr. V woke up on the wrong side of the bed this morning," replied Lynn.

"Come on guys, give Mr. V a break, you know Mr. Vs not a morning person," said Chip.

"That's Chip," responded Buster, "always standing up for the underdog! Mr. Goodie Two Shoes! Oh, well, not much longer. This is your last week Chippie baby! Who's gonna stand up for Mr. V when Chippie boy's leaves?"

Even Oliver chuckled a bit with his laugh reminicent of the Penguin from Batman. But Chip looked at me and just shook his head.

So upon completion of the carriers inspecting their vehicles we proceeded to go back inside the building.

0735: The carriers report to their assigned cases and begin sorting the mail into the various address slots. At this time I also walk the around to each carrier and give them their daily instructions for the day. Such instructions consist of assisting other carriers on their routes, carrying segments of other routes that may not have a carrier assigned to it for that given day. I inform them of what time they should be finished casing the mail and heading out to delivers the mail and routes for the given day. During this time I will encounter employees who vehemently disagree with the instructions I give them. Others will say “Yeah right, whatever,” while others will simply nod their heads and agree. Most times my instructions are met with an attitude. Whatever the case it is this time that I go around to every carrier and give them their instructions for the day For example; “Good morning John, today you have approximately six feet of mail to sort. So you should be pulling down your route at nine o’clock and leaving for the street at nine fifteen. You will have a thirty-minute pivot on route ten and you should be done in eight hours today. Have a good one!”

It’s at this point that some carriers will just say okay. Some might say well “I have a lot of parcels and ten certified letters that will require me to go into overtime so I’m not going to be able to do the pivot.” A few will say “I don’t think so.” While others just laugh and say “Whatever you say, boss!”

0745: Carriers are casing mail. Clerks are sorting packages/parcels into hampers for the carriers to deliver on the street. Clerks are also sorting mail into what is known as the P.O. Box section for customer’s that have P.O. Boxes and thus do not get mail delivery to their homes.

“Well, guys, today is Wednesday, it’s hump day!” shouted Lynn.

“Hump day? I wish I could hump on you Lynn!” blurted out Marlon.

"Yeah!"

"Oh, you little guys are so nasty."

"Yeah, like dem little dogs…always humpin' on somebody's leg."

"Yeah, yelled out Zakar!"

"Oh, Marlon, you know what I meant," replied Lynn, "I meant it's hump day as in the middle of the work week."

"Yeah, Marlon, not like hump on her." responded Old Man.

Marlon smiled and said, "You can't blame me for trying."

The telephone rings: "Good morning Creeks Bend Post Office Mr. V speaking may I help you?"

"Yes, I hope so. I live in a community where we have one of those multi-unit boxes that like stand on a column or a pedestal. You know what I mean?" she asked.

"Yes, I do." I replied.

"Okay good. Well, my husband lost our mailbox keys and now we can't get into our box and I'm wondering how we can get our mail."

"Okay, are you sure you lost both sets of keys?" I asked. "You should have received a spare key when you first were given the box."

"Yes, I'm sure. Neither my husband nor I can find it. Unfortunately, that was our spare key. We lost the other key about a year ago."

"Well, in that case, we will have to change your lock and provide you with new keys."

"Okay, that's fine. Is there a fee or a charge for that?"

"Yes, it's twenty-five dollars."

"Okay, well I guess there's no way around that."

"No, I'm sorry there's not."

"Okay, when can I expect this to be done?"

"Well, I will let our custodian know and they should be able to fix it this afternoon. What is your name and address." I asked her So I after she provided the necessary information, I informed her that once the lock had been changed we would give her a call and that she could come to the post office to pay for the service and pick up the new keys. As she was satisfied with the outcome of our conversation and we both hung up our phones.

The telephone rings again! I let it ring a couple times to see if Meghyn might pick it up. I answer on the third ring.

"Good morning, Creeks Bend Post Office, Mr. V speaking may I help you?"

"Yes, I have not received my last two bank statements from my bank and I am very concerned as they contain personal information regarding my accounts and social security number. Now I did call the bank and they assured me that they had mailed both of them out and they confirmed my address as well. So I was hoping you could tell me where they were." I pause and think to sarcastically say to myself, *Oh sure right, I know exactly where your statements are.* They're right here in my hands. I proceeded to ask for his information before informing him that I was going to place him on hold and speak with the carrier who delivers his mail.

He then said to me, "Yes, please do because I'm really concerned about these statements especially with so much identity theft going on these days."

"Yes, sir I understand. Well, may I please place you on hold? I will be right back?"."

"Yes, you may." he answered.

After placing the man on hold a few moments and talking with the carrier, I discovered that the gentleman's son, who happened to have the same identical name, recently moved out of the house and had submitted a "Change of Address" as he had moved out of town to another state. So when the regular carrier was off the substitute carrier, in error, had forwarded the bank statements not realizing that there were two individuals in the same house with the same first, middle and last names with Sr. and Jr. being the only difference. Apparently, the mail in question did not designate Sr. or Jr.

I returned to the phone and informed the gentleman what had happened with his mail. He was a little upset but understood the process. I let him know that the mail was most likely sent to his son or even perhaps returned to the sender. So I advised him to check with his son. End of that conversation!

I typically may answer a few calls like this throughout the day.

As always, there are several conversations between employees going on the workroom floor. Sometimes the postmaster will page me over the intercom, "Mr. V. it's pretty loud out there. Please quiet them down." Whenever I tell the employees to quiet down they immediately respond "Oh, so now we can't talk?" I advise them, "No you can talk: it's just that you are talking too loud." This is a daily battle!

0750: I hear a cell phone ring. It's Lynn. She quietly answers the phone and whispers to her boyfriend named Bo, "I can't talk right now but I will call you back in a minute."

She looks at me with her eyebrows raised as if to say, Yes can I help you? She then proceeds to walk to the women's restroom. As she does, I hear Reds exclaim, "Geez Lynn isn't it a little early for a booty call?"

"Yeah," shouted Zakar!

Lynn just made a face and stuck her tongue at him as she continued to walk away from her case to the woman's room.

Reds then replied, "You shouldn't stick your tongue out unless you plan to use it."

"Yeah, hollered Marlon!"

"Let me know when you're ready buddy boy," replied Lynn.

"Hey, watch your mouth," said Rico.

"Yeah, again shouted Zakar!"

"Oh, that's so gross," said Oliver.

"Yeah," hollered Marlon again.

0752: Lynn is in the women's restroom returning the call to her boyfriend Bo. The following conversation was overheard by Samantha. Samantha happened to be in the women's room at the same time and was peaking through the stall listening to, and watching Lynn. Oddly enough, Lynn never knew Samantha was in there.

"Hey, pretty boy, I just had this feeling you might call this morning. What's going on, asked Lynn? What? Meet you at twelve-thirty today? Well,…sure! Where? Oh, my! You mean behind the abandoned warehouse, right? Ummm, what do you have in mind baby? Oooh, I love it when you talk like that… Mmm…it makes me tingle."

She takes her left hand and gently caresses her neck.

"Hey," she continues, "I just remembered that you're off today. Good for you. What vehicle will you be in? Oh~ the van machine? Yeah, I know, I really enjoyed you the other night too. Actually, baby, I enjoyed us! You make me feel a way that I haven't felt in a long time. Oh, by the way, did your wife say anything to you when you came home the other night? Oh, honey, I know how that bothers you, you know coming home every night and finding her there spread out on the floor with beer cans laying around. She's such a drunk. You deserve so much better. I feel so sorry for you. Well, listen I gotta get back to my case, I'm sure my ***stupidvisor*** is looking for me. But I really look forward to seeing you about twelve-thirty today…my heart is already pounding! I can't wait. Oh, and bring a couple of extra blankets or quilts with you okay? You know I like being cozy and all. I love you, big boy!"

Lynn then stops to use the restroom and stays in the restroom a few minutes longer.

Samantha remained quiet as a church mouse the entire time and did not come out of the women's room until well after Lynn had finished and left. She did not want Lynn to know she had overheard her conversation. Samantha actually told me this story some weeks later.

Mean while back out on the workroom floor, Marlon yelled out to me.

"Hey, Mr. V!"

"I'm busy!" I said in return.

"Yeah, right you ain't busy."

"Yeah, can't you see Mr. V is busy sitting at his desk, said Old Man."
"Mr. V, how long is Lynn gonna stay in the ladies room, asked Marlon?"

"Yeah, how long, chimed in Reds?"

I heard them but I did not respond.

0802: Buster leaves his case, with a newspaper in hand, to go to the men's room.

"Hey, where's he going," asked Zakar?

"Don't you worry where I'm going youngster," replied Buster.
"Maybe he's gonna join Lynn in the ladies room." said Oliver.

"Yeah!"

0809: Buster comes out of the men's restroom. "Ummm, that was something, Shoo-ee! I pity the fool who goes in that stall after me."

"Was it that bad Buster?" asked Marlon.

"Heck yeah, it was that bad. What you think I enjoyed being in there. Now I know why they call it the crapper."

"Why do they call it the crapper Buster?" asked Rico.

"Cause when you are in there and you smell that mess the only thing you can say is OH CRRRAP!" replied Buster. Buster continues, "Hey, Rico, I know with the food you Puerto Ricans eat, it's gotta stink up in there! All those refried beans, pork, jalapenos and Spanish rice. Man, you couldn't pay me to eat that mess!"

"Yeah," quipped Marlon.

Everyone started laughing. Rico just shook his head.

Chip pipped up, "Hey, Rico, don't worry, I like your food, it just doesn't like me."

"Hey, you think Spanish food is hot, you should try Indian food." responded Oliver. "Now that food is spicy. It goes in hot and comes out even hotter! It'll make you want to sit on a hose."

"Hey, Oliver, you should be used to that, I hear you like sitting on hoses," chimed Zakar.

"Hahaha, yeah," responded Marlon with a laugh.

"Hey, hey, hey you guys, now you know that's not right," responded Rico.

"Yeah!"

0810: Buster, realizing that Lynn has not returned from the ladies room asks, "Hey, where is Lynn? She's not back yet? Damn, what she doing in there? You know she's gonna say she won't be able to complete her route in eight hours and she's gonna ask for assistance or overtime!"

Willie asked, "Wow she's still in the restroom?

"Yeah, she's still in there!"

"- Uhhh, maybe somebody oughtta go and check on her," said Old Man.

"Yeah, maybe someone like me," said Willie.

Reds blurted out, "That's my boy Willie! Hey, Old Man, how does that Elvis Presley song go? 'You ain't nuttin but a hound dog.'"

"Yeah, right, I can see it now…Buster is just gonna stroll into the ladies room and yell, LYNN ARE YOU OK?" exclaimed Chip.

"No way! I ain't gonna walk in there. You know women can stink up a place just as bad as a man. It ain't just the men," replied Buster. "Shoot, my grandmother, God rest her soul, used to run her old man outta the house!"

"Her old man, why did you say her old man," asked Chip, "wasn't that your grandfather?"

"Yeah," exclaimed Marlon.

"Heck no! My grandmother's husband died years ago. I loved that cat! But then she remarried. So he's not my grandfather." explained Buster.

0812: While they were continuing on in their conversation Lynn exited the restroom. As she did, Reds teased…"Well, look who it is…hey, Lynn, where you been?"

"Yeah, where ya been Lynnie," questioned Zakar?"

Lynn quietly walked back to her mail case as if she knew she had been in the ladies room longer than usual. I approach her and ask, "Lynn you were away from your case a long time. Are you okay… is everything okay?" I asked faking my concern.

"Uh, let's see, Mr. V…I guess I had to go the ladies room."

"You were in there quite a long time, at least twenty minutes."

"Oh, really? I didn't know I was on a timer. Don't you think that's a bit of harassment, Mr. V?" she asked. "Uh huh, well anyway Mr. V, I'm on my period and I'm not having a good day. I can show you if you really need to see." she replied in an elevated tone as she attempted to stare me down.

"Oh, my God, did you guys hear that? That is so nasty." said Oliver with a cringe.

Reds shuddered, bending over at the waist laughing and hooted, "Oh I can't believe she said that."

"Oh, well, she might be a woman but she's no lady," responded Buster.

All eyes fell on me as they awaited my reaction. Conceding but not convinced I say, "No Lynn, I really don't think you need to show me anything." I turned away from her in disgust and start to walk back to the supervisor desk."

"Yeah, well fine! And oh, by the way, Mr. V, I'm going to need about thirty minutes street help to make it back in eight hours so I will be giving you a request for assistance form, I'm really not feeling all that well…you should be glad I'm not going out sick," she responded as she spun away from me, proceeding to pick up a handful of letters and resumed casing her mail.

"I guess that's why you get paid the big bucks, Mr. V." stated Reds with that sarcastic grin.

"Yeah, Mr. V gets paid the big bucks," exclaimed Willie!

"Yeah," shouted Marlon.

"Oh, yeah right, I get paid the *BIG* bucks," sarcastically I replied " Shoo-ee, eh, uh, these letters are kinda stiff today! How about you Reds, do you have a lotta letters today?" asked Willie. "Man, I don't think I can make it back in time either Mr. V! Heck I might need an extra thirty minutes myself."

"WHAAAT? What do you mean you might need an extra thirty minutes. You oughtta be glad you gotta job! Boy, you people are something else." cried Old Man. "I remember back in the day when we had to case two to three trays of letters every day. Now with everything being run on machines we only gotta case maybe eight to twelve inches of letters nowadays. You people are something, all you do is complain."

"Old Man is right…some of you people should be glad you have a job." echoed Chip.

"Uh oh, there you guys go again with that *YOU PEOPLE* mess. You all ain't nuttin but a bunch of rednecks up in this place. Ain't nuttin changed since slavery, it's just more subtle." responded Buster.

"Hey, Willie, whatcha gonna do with all that overtime money you been making," inquired Reds.

"Maybe he'll finally pay back all that money Old Man loaned him two years ago," said Rico.

"Yeah, right, that'll be the day." Old Man said in a smart-alec tone.

"Huh, I bet his landlord hopes he'll be able to pay next months rent," shouted Marlon.

"Hahaha, very funny, very funny." retorted Willie.

"Oh, my, you gotta love this place." sniggered Reds.

"Can you believe that Chip?" Rico asked. "This guy has been in the post office over thirty years and he still has trouble paying his rent. He's still borrowing off people."

"I know, it's like what does he do with his money?" Chip quizzed.

"You know the deal Chip, there's only one answer…WOMEN! He spends it all on women, trying to be Mr. Big Shot," answered Rico.

"Hey, guys come on, can't we all just get along?!" shouted Reds.

“Oh, here we go, Mr. Rodney King impersonator!” Buster mocked.

“Yeah,” replied Zakar

“Yeah, Reds, *Mr. Can't We All Just Get Along?* We can all get along until it’s something you don’t like, and then you wanna hate the world. I’ve never seen a person who can be as bipolar as you Reds.” Lynn spat.

“Yeah! We have one person who’s bipolar and another person who’s bisexual. Looks like the bi’s rule around here.” responded Marlon.

“Yeah,” replied Zakar once again.

“Mr. V, ya just gotta keep praying for these people. Hopefully, God will have mercy on their souls.” said Rico.

“All right that’s far enough guys. No talking about God in the post office…let’s keep religion out of it.” responded Old Man.

“Yeah, guys that’s right. This is a God-free zone here” said Oliver.

“What’s a God-free zone? Now I heard it all! Is that like a no smoking zone?” Chip interjected.

“Yeah, didn’t you see the sign when you first started working here?It read, ‘Talking about God in the post office is strictly prohibited.’” insisted Oliver.

"Oh, come on Oliver," responded Rico, "you know you ain't never seen a sign like that up in here!"

"Well, how about separation of church and state?" Oliver responded.

"Hey, Oliver, I don't think the post office qualifies as a church. And besides, we're government employees, not state employees." said Marlon.

"Hahahahah! Boy that Marlon is quite a character." Lynn giggled.

"Yeah, Oliver! We can't talk about the Man Upstairs but it's okay for you to talk about the men you've slept with! I'm out." shouted Buster.

"Hey, hey," shouted Rico, "watch that!"

"Yeah, but it's not okay for someone to talk about how praying to God has helped them," said Rico. "You people are something. You always want to exclude God out of your lives until a tragedy occurs and then you will start asking, where is God?"

"Amen, brother that's right. You hit the nail on the head." agreed Chip.

"Yeah," hollered Reds, "Preach that, Rico!"

"Yeah, preach that Reverend Rico," echoed Willie!

"Hey, Rico, how about saying a prayer for me?" Lynn requested.

"Hey, Lynn, I can say a prayer for you honey," said Willie. "I'll pray that you'll give me one of those full frontal hugs like you gave Oliver the other day. Come on sugar, just once, you know there's no shame to my game baby." laughed Willie.

"Neeever gonna get it, neeever gonna get it," sang Lynn.
"Yeah, you ain't neeever gonna get it. Heck, I stand a much better chance than all ya'll." expressed Marlon!

"You go on and get it handsome!" shouted Old Man.

"Neeever gonna get it, neeever gonna get it," Lynn repeated.

"Yeah, little man, da bouf of you got little ones, I'M OUT! Now me on the other hand…I'm the right man for the job! Ain't that right Lynn?" provoked Buster!

"Neeever gonna get it, neeever gonnna get it!"

Chip just started laughing.

"Ahh shut up, Mr. Goodie Two Shoes!" commanded Buster.

"Hey, Moe," said Katie passing by.

"Hey, Curly," I replied.

"Hey, Porcupine," shouted Old Man!

0814: Oliver hurriedly goes to the men's room. I start to get up from my chair to see what was wrong with him as everyone looks on.

0815: Telephone rings…

"Saved by the bell again Oliver." yelled Old Man.

"Yeah, all that bisexual talk must have stimulated him….hahaha." snorted Zakar.

"Good morning Creeks Bend post office Mr. V. speaking may I help you?"

"Yes, I was hoping you could help me."

"Okay, how can I help you?" I inquire.

"Yes, I went to your postal website to track a package that was mailed to me five days ago. I requested your expedited service because I needed the item right away. However, according to tracking I see that the package arrived at your local unit two days ago. It says a notice was left, which I did not get because I don't live there anymore as I recently moved to the next town over. Then the tracking information says that the item was forwarded. Well, I like to know when I will receive this package? It's very important to me and I needed it two days ago! That's why I requested the expedited service. So I'd like to know when I'm going to receive it!"

"Well, sir, you should receive the package in two to three business days."

"Two to three more business days, that's unacceptable I need the item right away, it's already late!" the man exasperatedly countered.

"Excuse me sir but did you say you had recently moved?"

"Yes, I did!"

"Well, why didn't you have the package sent directly to your new address as opposed to it being sent here?"

"Yeah, yeah yeah, my wife asked me the same thing."

"Well, I'm sorry sir but per your request, the item was forwarded to the new address you provided. However, once it is forwarded it gets sent to our processing and distribution plant where it will be redirected to your new local post office and address."

"You mean to tell me," responded the gentleman, "that you folks sent my package all the way down to some plant out of town when I only moved to the next town down the road from you guys? My goodness, you could have walked it to me or even called me and I could have come down there to pick it up! Well, I want my money back for the extra service I requested and not given!"

"I'm sorry sir but we cannot honor the extra service requested by you as the package did arrive here in time. And because of your new forwarding change of address submitted by you, it will now take longer."

"Well, some kind of service that is! That's one hell of a way to run a business! I want the money back that I paid for the extra service! What time does your office close?"

"Our office is open 'til five o' clock."

"I will be down there today and I **better** get some satisfaction! What an operation you idiots run down there? This is not the first time that I have had problems with you people! What's your position?"

"I'm a supervisor, not an idiot," I professionally retorted.

"Yeah, right…you could've fooled me. I guess you're in the union too." he stated.

"I'm sorry sir, I know the system doesn't make sense but that's how the operation runs."

"Well, apparently not only does it not make sense, it's obviously not making money either. It's no wonder you people are losing money by the billions!"

"Again, I'm sorry sir. Is there anything else I can do for you?"

"How can you help me now?" he replied, "It's too late now!" *Click!*

"Hey Mr. V, sounds like another satisfied customer," tauntedWillie as he chuckled.

"Mr. V!" shouts Reds, "Since you're our delivery specialist, perhaps you can tell me why I just received this envelope that's post dated the fourteenth and today is now the twentieth? I mean that's six days according to my calculations. Hey it was only mailed out of Philadelphia. I think Philly's only forty-five minutes away."

"I don't know Reds, could be a number of reasons," I replied.

"So what am I to tell my customer," he asked?

"I don't know Rick," I repeat.

"Well, what do you know? No wonder the post office is losing money…we can't even deliver the mail across town in a timely manner. I'll tell you what Mr. V. I will have the customer call you when they ask me why it took so long. I will give them your name specifically. Perhaps you can say to 'em "I don't know."

"Uh oh, sounds like the sleeping bear has awakened from his den." instigated Chip.

"Yeah, I know Chip, of all the letters that get delivered in a timely manner, there had to be one that did not and of course it would be on Reds' route" commented Old Man.

"Yeah, Reds doesn't miss a thing." said Zakar.

"Yeah, you're right I don't miss a thing. You just make sure you don't miss scanning another package!"

" Ooooh, that was a good one Reds. You're so perfect! It must be nice to never make mistake. You're always bringing up somebody's errors." returned Zakar.

"Yeah, that's right," said Reds, "and just remember Zakar…I can be your best friend or your worst enemy."

"Al salam a lickem brother," shouted Marlon as he intentionally mispronounced the saying.

"Hey, watch your mouth! Leave my religion out of this," Replied Zakar.

"Religion, heck, I got you all beat. I was an alter boy! Yeah, how bout that. I carried the candles at mass." said Marlon.

"Yeah, and I bet you dropped wax all over the altar too." shouted Buster!

"Yeah, right, good one!"

0820: Meghyn paged me on the intercom. 'V, intercom ten please!"

"I'm busy!"

"Uh oh Mr. V, what did you do now?" asked Old Man.

I made her wait about a minute and then picked up the phone to intercom her back.

"Hello V?"

"Y-yyes?"

"Have you taken Habib into the office yet? I want to make sure you issue him his letter of discipline. You know my boss wants us to take corrective action. Especially since this customer had called Headquarters to file a formal complaint."

"Yes, I was just about to take him when you paged me."

"Okay great, you da man V!"

I call Habib into the office with his union shop steward and issue him a Notice of seven-day Paper Suspension for Failing to Follow Instructions. Just yesterday he, once again, mis-delivered a package containing medication, to an address where the package did not belong instead of delivering to the address on the package. The postal customer had brought the package to us late, yesterday afternoon so that we could get it to the correct recipient and they would have their medication. Habib constantly makes such errors. Just three days ago I received a call from one of his postal customer's and the man laid me out for allowing such a person to work at the post office. I had already taken him in the office for that. This is not the first time this customer has called.

"Habib this is a Pre-disciplinary Investigation that may result in corrective action being taken against you for "Unacceptable Performance". Again, just yesterday you mis-delivered another letter belonging to Mr. Gino at 919 Tree Lane to 919 Boulder Drive. Habib, the customer was very irate! You keep missing deliveries! Not only his mail but mail belonging to other customers. What do you have to say about this?"

Habib simply replied, "Yeah yeah yeah I know. I will pay more attention."

"Yes, I know you are going to pay more attention because I have had it up to here with your unacceptable performance! You've got to pay more attention to the mail. You can't just grab a bundle of mail, not look at it, and throw it into the customer's mailbox without first looking at it and making sure it's the right mail for the residence you're at. I told you before, you must finger through each piece of mail before placing it into the mailbox. Now I asked you before, do you feel you need more training?"

"No, I don't need more training."

"Are you sure Habib?"

"Yes, Mr. V, I'm sure"

"Does this mean that you are going to issue Habib a Letter of Warning for this?" asked Gino, the union shop steward.

"Well I have to investigate it more. However, I must inform you that since this is hardly the first time and since we've already been down the road of official discussions, which do not seem to be working, this incident may indeed warrant corrective action, Gino! But again, I have to do my investigation and think about it."

Gino turns to Habib and says, "Habib you've got to slow down and pay more attention. You have to be more careful."

"Yes, I know, I know. I will pay more attention." he replied.

I inform both Habib and Gino that they could return back to their cases and to continue casing up their mail. At that point, the Pre-disciplinary Investigation was over.

As I walked out of the office, I hear Reds say "Looks like the terrorist is up to his old ways again."

Chip replied by saying, "Reds, you are such a redneck!"

"Yeah, why you think we call him Reds," shouted Marlon.

0828: It's time to give the daily safety talk over the intercom.

Daily safety talks and informational messages are communicated over the telephone speaker to all employees while they are performing their daily tasks. Sometimes I may call all employees to the middle of the workroom when more emphasis is needed.

I begin the announcement," The subject matter today deals with following too closely to the vehicle in front of you or tailgating." "Always allow approximately three to four seconds between you and the car in front of you as this will allow the ample braking and stopping time needed." Due to a recent accident experienced by one of our postal employees I add, "When stopped at a traffic light or stop sign, if you can not see the bottom of the wheels of the vehicle in front of you on the ground then you are too close to that vehicle. Should that vehicle start to pull away and suddenly stop you could rear end them. If you follow these simple and basic rules when driving then everything will be alright!"

So I document the safety talk and staple it to my daily paperwork.

Meghyn, the postmaster, and I talk about the value of having such talks documented, especially if the office should experience a preventable accident. It ensures that we can show evidence that daily safety talks are given and employees constantly refreshed on safe driving principles. Should one of our employees be involved in an accident and one or both of us has to appear before a safety review board.

This is also when I will give a service talk. This particular talk is about scanning packages; the value and benefits to both the sender and the end customer. "Carriers, please make sure that you are appropriately scanning all scannable items whether it is attempted, undeliverable as addressed or delivered. This process lets the customer know where their packages are as today's customer is information driven. It's also a revenue stream that we need to capture as our first-class mail continues to decline due to the internet. If we want to build this business, continue getting our paychecks and make sure we all will have pensions when we retire, we must successfully capture this growing segment of the mailing industry."

0830: "City carriers, I continued, it's time for the ten-minute city carrier office break. Please return back to your cases in ten minutes. RD carrier's, you keep working." Some of the city carriers laughed.

0830 – 0840: Carriers take the first of their two ten minute breaks. At our office, the first break is taken in the office and the second break is taken on the street. Employees are also entitled to a thirty-minute lunch break. I tell the carriers, "According to the clock over route 1 the time is now eight thirty, straight up. Therefore you are to be back at your cases and working at eight forty." Some carriers go outside or will go into the swing room. A few carriers will gather at one of the routes directly behind the supervisor's desk, where I sit and chat. Some of the chatting consists of complaining about management, the postal system, or simply whatever the latest current events in the news are.

Note: Throughout the day I will take calls from customers. Such calls range from inquiries about; obtaining passports, complaints of mis-deliveries, no delivery, complaints about mail pieces being received in damaged condition and possible lost mail. Such calls, or complaints for me anyway, are draining and annoying. You would be surprised how often the phone rings. You'd think we were "The Bell Telephone Company" or something.

0841: Telephone rings; it's a customer calling to have their mail put on hold for several days.

"Good morning, Creeks Bend post office, Mr. V. speaking may I help you?"

Customer responds, "Yes, perhaps you can help me. I will be going out of town few a few days and I would like my mail to be held at your office until I return."

"When will you be leaving?

"Tomorrow morning." the customer says.

"Sure we can do that for you. However, for your protection, we would like to have that in writing. You can simply go to our website and submit a Hold My Mail request, or if you like you may leave a note in your mailbox for your postman and when he delivers your mail today he will pick up the note."

"Okay, if that's it I will leave the note in the box. What should the note say?"

I advise to write their name, address, and the day they want their hold to begin. As well as the day they would like their mail delivery to resume. I instruct them further to write on the note, Per my authorization please hold my mail and sign and date it.

"Okay great, thank you for your help," says the customer before hanging up.

0842: Telephone rings; it's another customer calling to see if an item is still here at the post office.

"Good morning, Creeks Bend post office, Mr. V. speaking can I help you?"

"Yes," says the customer, "I received a note in my mailbox yesterday saying 'Sorry that we missed you' I was just checking to see if it was there and I could get a redelivery of it?"

"Okay, can you please give me your name and address…thank you… and can you tell me if the note says whether it's a letter or parcel?"

"Let me see." Oh the note says parcel."

"Okay sir, may I put you on hold while I check for your item?"

"Yes, that's fine," replies the man.

"Okay I'm back, thank you for holding, your parcel is available for pick up, would you like for it to be redelivered or will you come in today to pick it up?"

"Let's see, I may not be home all day so I will come in to pick it up."

"No problem, Sir. We are open until five o'clock PM, you may come in to pick it up anytime between now and then."

"Okay, sounds great I will see you later today!" says the customer, disconnecting the call.

0843: Meghyn pages me…"V, intercom ten please!"

"I'm busy!" I responded. Reds kinda chuckles.

I pick up the phone…"Yes Meghyn?"

"Is everybody going to be back on time today," she asks?

"Yes, everyone should be back on time."

"Okay good,". What are your total hours for today, I have to report them to my boss?"

I tell her the hours and hang up. I overhear Reds say "So she beat you up again huh Mr. V?" I just look at him with a puzzled look. There are people in the post office who really enjoy what they may believe to be another person's misery.

Marlon shouts across the workroom floor to Zakar.

"Hey, Zakar you shoulda seen what Mindy the desk clerk had on yesterday at the hair care and spa salon!"
"You mean the Bold N Brash?"

"Yeah!"

"What, what, tell me…what did she have on…or better yet, what didn't she have on?" asked Zakar.

"I don't know what you call it but it might as well had been nuttin. Oh, my god…I mean I could see everything! My eyes must have been as big as cantaloupes. I almost forgot to pick up the outgoing mail from off her desk I was looking so hard."

"Oh, Marlon is such a pervert." sighed Oliver.

"Hahahaha! Did you all hear Oliver? He's such a pervert," mimicked Buster.

"Boy, I bet that's your favorite delivery stop of the day, eh Marlon?" asked Old Man.

"You know it is." said Lynn

"Hey, don't tell Meghyn, but I go in there at least twice a day. I mean I could stay in there all day and just watch the women, especially on Fridays!"

"Fridays…why Fridays," asked Chip?

"Because it's their dress down day and they really dress down, if you know what I mean?" smiled Marlon.

"Yeah!"

"What kind of services do they offer there?"

"You know all the usual stuff like getting your hair done, your nails, your foot nails."

"You mean pedicures!"

"What you mean like dogs and cats pet cures?" probed Oliver'

"No Oliver, pedicures as in feet!" cackled Chip

"Hey, Oliver, see my thumb, gee your stupid." snipped Marlon.

“No Marlon, the saying goes like this…see my thumb, boy you’re dumb!” corrected Lynn.

“Yeah, who’s the dumber, Marlon or Oliver?”

“Oh, good one!” sneered Marlon!

“Do they give massages there too?” asked Old Man.

“Yes, they do Old Man, but as old as you are I don’t think it would benefit you. Anyway, you’d probably get a heart attack.” joked Marlon.

“Very funny, young man…very funny!”

“Hey, I think I might get one of dem massages. I think you can even take your clothes off. I’d be naked! Hey, do you think they would massage my front too?” asked Marlon.

“Oooo, little man, you’re so nasty!” Buster wisecracked..

“That’s Marlon the lover boy at his best!” quipped Lynn.

“Hey, Marlon, I thought you were married?” Rico questioned.

“Yeah!”

“Rico, Marlon might be married but he’s not DEAD!” Chip kiddingly said.

"Yeah!"

0844: Chip, carrier route number five, looked a little wobbly and queasy. He sat down on the stool at his case. I approached and checked if he felt okay.

He reassured me, "Yes, I'll be okay, I just felt a little dizzy."

"You mean like vertigo?"

"Yes. Actually, I've been feeling like this on and off all week. It's probably just anxiety about my retiring as well as my daughter Carly getting married. But don't you worry Mr. V, I'll be okay!"

"Chip looked a little pale to me."

Chip is a twentyoneyear postal employee along with twenty years of active and Honorable military service in the U.S. Marines, prior to coming to the post office. He retired as a Corporal. Chip, after all these years, is still on the 12 hour Overtime Desired List (ODL) believe it or not. Reason being that he both needs and wants the extra money that being on the overtime desired list can provide. His daughter is getting married in two weeks. ODL people desire to work their Scheduled Day Off SDO and are willing to work up to 12 hours per day if needed. Working the SDO is where the overtime money is. It's a time and a half rate. I believe he made nearly seventyeight thousand dollars last year which is twentytwo thousand more than his base pay.

Chip is very neat in appearance, methodical and very detail oriented. He says it's because of his military background. The delivery route he has is known as a retirement route because the route is easy with no walking, and the customer's who live on his route are mostly age fifty-five or older. Essentially, it is known as an adult community for residents fifty five years in age and older. Being mostly retirees with well to do retirement incomes, it generates a lot of mail volume; especially during the fall mailing season. It's during this time of the year that there is plenty of overtime to be made on his route alone. Additionally, Chip can make a lot of overtime during the summer months as well by working his non-scheduled day off.

His mail route is in the nice part of our delivery area. All of Chip's customers love him because of his neatness. He also goes out of his way to spoil them with personal outstanding service, like doing little favors. Of course, during the Christmas Holiday, he makes out like a bandit with the Christmas tips. He's basically an all around good employee with a very pleasant attitude and personality. However, I think he milks the route a little bit to make overtime. I think most of the carriers could work a little faster but then again there are no real performance standards which they have to meet. That, in my opinion is anti-productive. In the post office, it is well known that the slugs make the money. The hustler only gets more work.

Nevertheless, after a few minutes, a calm chat between the two of us, and several sips of his coffee, Chip gathered himself and slowly stood back up to continue his work. Everything appeared alright and he guaranteed me that he was okay. Chip suffers from Hypertension but is very good about taking his medication and getting his yearly physicals. He also watches his weight very well.

After that I walked back over to my desk, sat down, took a deep breath and continued my daily reports.

As soon as I take my seat, Meghyn walks over to me and asks;

"Hey, V, what is Oliver doing over there? Looks like he's casing the mail as if it's the first time he's seen the case! V, you need to do something with him, take him in the office or something...he's killing us!"

Immediately I get up from my chair and walk over to where Oliver is. I stand behind him and watch him case mail for awhile.

Of course, Reds eats that up. He then opens his mouth, "Hey, Mr. V, why don't you take my stool and sit there for awhile?"

Oliver then notices me, "Is something wrong Mr. V?"

"Yes, Oliver, you've been on this route now for two years and you still look like you don't have a clue where the addresses are! You're hunting and pecking like it's the first time you've seen the case. This is unacceptable."

I continue to observe him. It's not before long that Oliver becomes flatulent. Whenever he gets nervous and his stomach starts to rumble, his gas will betray him like stink on a skunk.

“Oh, my God,” gags Old Man. “Smells like Oliver is having bowel problems. Mr. V is standing behind him and Oliver is farting! Oh my eyes, my eyes are burning. Mr. V can’t you do something about him?! Oliver, you gotta get control of yourself, that smell is horrible!”

“I’m sorry guys, but you know I can’t take when Mr. V stands behind me like that. He’s watching me like a hawk,” said Oliver.

Plugging my nose I begin to head his way. “Oliver, it looks like you have no idea of what you’re doing. You like you have never cased mail on the route before! I mean look at you, you’re looking and searching all over the case! What’s the problem?”

“Mr. V…I don’t know,” as he looks down. “You know I get nervous when you guys stand behind me and watch me.”

“You guys! What do you mean by you guys? What, are you talking about the department store or something, ha, you guys.” grumbled Buster.

“Oh yeah, that’s right! Remember that department store? It was called Two Guys! Boy, that’s going back a few years.”

“Yeah, maybe he meant to say “You People!”

"Yeah, said Zakar!"

"No, no, no, I didn't mean you people." responded Oliver.

"Hahahahaha! Did you hear Oliver, no, no, no, I didn't mean you people. Oliver, you crack me up. Say that again Oliver, no, no, no!" Buster said as he burst into a laughing fit.
"Well, anyway, Mr. V, I've been having trouble with my eyes lately."

"Oliver, please come with me into the supervisor's office."

"Okay. Do I need my shop steward?" he asks.

"No, this is not a disciplinary related issue Oliver, however, we do need to talk…and besides, your noxic emissions are very offensive!"

Lynn in a consoling tone, "Poor Oliver. Oliver honey, remember, STAND TALL…don't let Mr. V intimidate you honey, STAND TALL!" she yells after him. Ironic as Oliver is a bit on the chubby side and is short in height, about 5'4".

Oliver just chuckles in his flamboyant voice, "Thank you Lynn, for the encouragement."

As we get closer to the office, Reds goes, "Hey, Mr. V why don't you just move Oliver's case into the office. That way it'll save you some walking time."

"Yeah!"

"You know how you managers are always so concerned about time efficiency and time wasting movements," continued Reds.

"Hey," blurted out Zakar, "Maybe instead of management being so obsessed with cutting our routes down, perhaps they can find a way to cut down on Oliver's and Mr. Vs travel time to the supervisor's office."

"I think that's what Reds was alluding to, dumb dumb!" responded Old Man.

"Oh, good one Old Man." shouted Zakar.

"Oh, shut up!" barks Buster. "All ya'll know the man can't see. You can see that by the way he cuts his hair. I'm out!" Oliver sports a moderate Mohawk style haircut.

"Yeah, yeah." says Marlon.

Lynn goes into mother hen mode as she quickly runs up to Oliver. "Oh, Oliver sweetie, do you need a hug? Come here baby, let me give you a huggy-huggy honey!"

Lynn loomed closer. Oliver quickly turned around and flung his hands up in the air pleading, "NO, NO…STOP!" However, Lynn prevailed in giving him a bear hug and pulling his head into her chest. Oliver breaks out of her grip and hurriedly runs into the men's room, forgetting that I had told him to come into the office with me. "There he goes, Mr. Neurotic, into the men's room to wash off!"

"Hey, I wonder what Oliver's more afraid of," Marlon pondered aloud, "catching germs or that he might start to like being hugged by a woman."

"Yeah!"

Besides suffering from Shingles, Oliver has a compulsive disorder and as such is really neurotic about germs and people touching him.

With flirtatious jealousy, Willie cries, "Lynn, I sure wish you would hug me like that…wow…gee wiz! I mean I don't wanna be Oliver to have to get a hug like that,. But gosh, please tell me what I gotta do or who I need to be!"

Buster interjects, "You all are nothing but a bunch of ungodly perverts!"

"Geez Buster, is there such a thing as a godly pervert?" asked Old Man.

"Yeah, good one." said Zakar.

"Oh, shut up new school, you ain't been around here long enough to be chiming in on our conversation." said Buster, "I'll take you out back on the dock and wear your little so and so out."

"Yeah right," Zakar jeered "I'll bust a cap up your old ass."
"Hey, watch your mouth." shouted Rico.

"Whoa new school, you cats are violent…like Billy the Kid." Buster said trying to chill the feisty, young buck.

"Yeah." said Marlon.

"Brother V," chimed in Rico, "you really gotta pray for these people."

"Yeah!"

"Amen, HALLELUJAH! Rev. Rico…preach that thing! yelled Lynn.

"Hey, Mr. V, I thought you were gonna take Oliver into the office."

"Yeah! Now I guess Mr. V's gonna write him up for farting… Unacceptable Performance!" chuckled Reds.

Shaking my head, I head back to my desk, letting everyone's laughter trail behind.

"So you wanted to be a supervisor in the post office huh? Don't let them stress you out, boss." Reds called out.

0855: Carriers continue casing up the rest of their mail, obtain their Accountable Items from the Accountable Cart, which may be Certified or Registered letters as well as Overnight or Next Day packages. The Accountable Cart comes around to each carrier at his/her case. There also are customer's "Hold Mail Notices" to be given to the carriers as well as "Customer Pick-Up Request." A Customer Pick-Up Request is a request submitted by postal customers via the postal website. Customers simply click on the Customer Pick-Up Request button, enter their contact information, the day they want their items picked up and the number of packages to be picked up. Then they click the submit button and the post office receives the information the morning of the date entered.

0900: Some carriers begin pulling down their routes and loading their hampers. Buster has been fairly good all morning and steady at casing up all of his mail. The post office has just entered the Fall Mailing season and so the mail volume is on the increase as is typical for this time of year. The Fall Mailing season is when all mailers/retailers begin sending out their various catalogs in preparation for the holiday season. Such mailings of catalogs will run from mid-September until the first or second week of December. After that, the Christmas card volumes start increasing as well as the packages and parcels of various sizes.

Well, Buster starts to chatter and goes into his usual saying;

"Uhhh, I didn't mean to do all this, uh, Whoo, Shoo-ee, uh. I don't know what the rest of you Philistines have been doing all morning… but all I EVER do is work, work, work, work, work!"

Zakar agreed, "Yeah, me too, Buster, me too!"

"All shut up…who asked you? Talking about some me too, who is me too, what are you Chinese or something? Huh, me too. All ya'll oughtta stop stealing from the government with those little routes!I'm out!"

Zakar claps back, "Hey, you wanna piece of me?"

Buster heckled, "Boy, I'll hit you so hard you'll curse the day your daddy got your momma pregnant."

"Oh, good one." Zakar's attitude peppering his words.

"Yeah, good one." instigated Marlon.

"Alright guys, I said, let's keep it down, there are customer's standing at the retail window."

Buster caved in, "Okay witness, okay!"

0900-1000: This time period sometimes requires me to, and often deal with issues of misconduct, employee's attendance issues if they fail to report to work as scheduled, or issues of employees failing to follow Standard Operating Procedures (SOPs) or simply, follow instructions. Such meeting or discussions are called Pre-disciplinary Investigations (PDIs) and often will result in a formal discussion being given. Sometimes they result in some sort of corrective or disciplinary action being taken against an individual in hopes of correcting an area of performance. These meetings will almost always involve a union official, the Shop Steward. Such meetings can get heated.

0905: Telephone rings. I pick it up on the second ring. A goal of the post office to answer all phone calls within three rings. "Good morning, Creeks Bend Post Office, may I help you?"

"Uh-uh-uh, are-are-are, weee gggoing to get mmmail today?" the caller stutters.

"Yes, if there's any mail for you, you will get it today." I answered.

"Oh oh, okay, umm, thank you!" Click!

This lady, calls every week and asks the same question.

0906: Telephone rings. "Good morning, Creeks Bend Post Office, may I help you?"

"Yes, I have been trying to get in touch with my mailman at the Riverside Post Office but all I get is a busy signal and the local phone number is not listed in the phone book. Do you have a phone number for them?"

"Ma'am I'm sorry for the frustration you've experienced in trying to reach that Post Office. Recently, the post office issued a Toll-Free number for customers to call. There, customer's can get up to date information regarding items they mailed as long as they have a tracking number, as well as answers to most questions. Nevertheless, I can give you that office's local number. It's 610-654-0987."

"Oh, great, you have been a big help, say's the caller, goodbye!" Click!

0907: Telephone rings. "Good morning, Creeks Bend Post Office, may I help you?"

"Yes, we will be temporarily moving away in seven days for approximately six months and I would like to know how I go about changing my address to my new temporary address."

"That's simple," I respond. "Do you have internet service, I asked?

"Yes, I do," she replied.

"Good…just go to our website postal.com and click on change my address and simply follow the instructions. Once you have input all pertinent information, just click submit and we will receive the transmission. We will begin forwarding your mail on the date you request."

"Oh, okay. But uh, please tell me, how does the forwarding process work? I mean what actually happens to my mail," she asked?

"Well, whenever your mailman receives a letter or magazine addressed to you for that particular address, they will then put it in a tray that will be sent to our mail processing center. Once at the mail processing center the letter or mail will either be sprayed by the mail machine with the new address. In some cases, the mail item might receive a yellow sticker on it indicating the new address."

"Oh, okay great! I always wondered how it worked," said the woman. "Is there a fee for this service or is it done for free?"

"Yes, there is a small fee so you will need a credit card to pay for it."

"Okay, that's no problem. Now, what would I need to do if I return back earlier than the end date I put in?" asked the customer?

"Just give us a call or let us know you plan on returning early and we will resume delivery to your physical residence. At that time we will ask you to fax us the request for our records. Or you may simply go to your nearest post office and fill out a new card canceling out the previous order. I’m sure the postal clerk there will be more than happy to assist you.”

“Okay, wow, you have been very helpful, thank you much!”

“You’re welcome. Is there anything else that I can help you with today ma’am?”

“No, I don’t think so, but thank you again and you have a nice day…goodbye!”

“Goodbye, ma’am.”

0910: Telephone rings. “Man, will this phone ever stop ringing?! I grumble.

I pick the phone up on the third ring.

“Good morning, Creeks Bend Post Office, Mr. V speaking, may I help you?

The caller responds; “Do you know what time I will get my mail delivery today, I’m expecting a very important package?”

“Well, ma’am, I need to know what your address is.”

“I live up in the Heights near the creek, and it’s the second house on the left with the white picket fence." replied the lady.

"Ma'am, I n-e-e-e-d an address."

"Oh, oh yes, of course, it's 111 Old Maid Lane."
"111 Old Maid Lane." I repeat back to her.

"Yes, 111 Old Maid Lane."

"Ma'am…we do not have an address of 111 Old Maid Lane in our town…Actually, we don't have an Old Maid Lane, Road, or Street for that matter."

"Well, I told you, young man, it's 111 Old Maid Lane. And this package is very important and I need it today. Do you know when my mailperson will be coming today?"

"Ma'am, again, we do not have a 111 Old Maid Lane in our delivery area nor do we have an Old Maid Street, Road or Blvd, and we certainly don't have a Heights section."

"Young man," snaps the lady, "I have been living here for 45 years and my mail has been coming to this address all this time! "

"Well, ma'am," I ask, what town do you live in?"

"Sir, I live in the same town as your post office!"

"And which post office is that ma'am," I asked?

"It's the post office that I just called and you picked up the phone!"

I begin to chuckle under my breath and ask, "Which post office did you call?"

"Alright young man, now you're playing games with me…I'm not getting anywhere with you. Is there someone else there with whom I may speak with?" asked the lady.

"I'm sorry ma'am," I reply half-heartedly.

"Stop calling me ma'am and get me someone else please!"

"Okay, I will. May I ask what your name is?"

"My name is Ms. Ethel Brightbill. My father was Rev. J.T. Brightbill III, perhaps you heard of him?" she asked.

"No Ms. Brightbill I never heard of your father."

"Well," she continued, "after my blessed dear mother passed away, he lived here with me until his passing five years ago." she added.

"I'm sorry to hear that." I stated.

"Yes, we both lived here at 111 Old Maid…"

"Yes, Ms. Brightbill," as I interrupted her, "you told me the address, but please, can you tell me what phone number you called?"
"Yes, I called the number we're on right now!"

Oh, my goodness… I whisper to myself… "I'm going to place you on hold and will have someone else assist you."

She then asks, "And will this someone else person help me…I really need this package?

"Please Ms. Brightbill, just say the phone number that you are trying to reach?" I beg.

"Alright let's see," she paused for a moment, "I think it is 610-288-0341."

"Well, ma'am," I say chuckling, "you dialed the wrong phone number. This is 610-299-0341.

"What?!" replied the lady," Oh heavens to betsy, I'm so very embarrassed…I'm so very sorry sir. You must think I'm an idiot."

"That's okay Ms. Brightbill those numbers are right next to each other, it's easy to do."

"Well, anyway, might you know where my package is and when may I expect it to arrive?"

"No, I don't know, I replied, but if you have the tracking number perhaps I can track it for you."

"Oh, okay, the tracking number, tracking number, hmmm let's see… What is that, she asked?"

"The tracking number is the number that should have been provided to you by the sender or shipper when you ordered the item. It's usually a sixteen digit number in length."

"Wow, sixteen! That's a REALLY big one!" she expressed surprised. "Are all of them that big in size?"

"No ma'am they're not." I responded.

"Oh, okay. But you said it's sixteen in length?" she asked again.

"No ma'am, I said it's sixteen digits or numbers in length." rolling my eyes.

"Oh, okay. Well, either way, that's a long one!"

"Yes, ma'am, yes it is." I quietly laugh.

"Well, I don't think I was given one. Oh, I don't know what to do now!"

"Wait, I'll tell you what I'm gonna do, I began to say to her, how about if you just give me your address again and I will put you on hold, and I will call the post office for you and see if your package might be there today for delivery."

"Oh no! Please don't put me on hold. I tell you what I will hang up and you can call me back with the information. I don't like it when someone puts me on hold. I guess I just don't like waiting."

"Okay, Ms. Brightbill, I won't put you on hold, just give me your phone number, hang up, and I will call you back."

"Oh, thank sir, God bless you, I can see that you're a very patient man, much like my dear late father was."

Chortling to myself, "You're welcome ma'am. I promise I will call you back as soon as I have some information for you, okay?"

"Yes, okay, I will wait for your call. I need this package right away."

"Just out of curiosity Ms. Brightbill, what does the package contain?"

"Well, it's a pair of new eyeglasses that I ordered while watching one of those infomercials on the television."

"Uh huh~, I see! Well, Ms. Brightbill, I will call you as soon as I have more information."

"And how long will that be?"

"I don't know ma'am but I will handle it as fast as I can."

"Thank you, young man. Goodbye!"

"Goodbye, Ms. Brightbill!"

As I hang up the phone I mumble under my breath, *"Old Maid Lane" what an appropriate address for her. She definitely is an old maid!"* Some of the carriers happened to overhear me.

Willie was the first to speak up, "Hey, Mr. V that wasn't nice, I thought you were a religious man!"

"You know how they are." says Lynn, "Praising God on Sunday and raising hell on Monday! Can somebody give me an amen?…Boom shack a lack a lack a, come tie my bow tie!"

"Oh, there goes Lynn, speaking in tongues." cooed Old Man.

"Hallelujah, sister Lynn!" said Reds.

"Praise the lawd sister…praise the lawd!" yelled Willie.

"Alright folks, let's keep the noise down, you know there are customers at the window. And you know Meghyn can hear you."

"Oh, there he goes, see you guys, now we're not allowed to talk." said Zakar.

"Yeah, Mr. V just gave us the gag order." uttered Marlon.

"Oh, come on now! Where did you hear me say you were not allowed to talk, huh? All I said was let's keep the noise down. Did anyone hear me say you could not talk?"

"Hey, Mr. V, now who's getting loud? Remember, there are customers at the front window. Can you please keep the noise down?" said Willie.

I walk back to my desk shaking my head.

"Mr. V, with this cast of characters, you couldn't pay me to do your job," said Chip.

0930: The PM/ Closing Supervisor arrives to work. Her name is Peg; however, all of the employees call her Ms. Peggy because she is on the chunky side weight wise.

Now Ms. Peggy is a real trip! She comes across as an elementary school teacher and will talk to you that way as well. I don't think she realizes it. Financially speaking Peggy is a well to do thirty-five-year-old Black woman married with two children. Her husband has a high end paying white collar job with a regional railway system. Peggy comes across as having an uppity and eccentric personality. Among other things she is well known for her daily greeting "Good morning Creeks Bend!" To which everyone will responds "Good morning Ms. Peggy!" Peggy wears cat eye glasses, changes her hair style every three months, and after having two children has gained about fifty pounds since I first met her. Basically, Ms. Peggy desperately needs a makeover. Come on Peggy, it's the year twenty-sixteen, not the sixties!

Unfortunately, Ms. Peggy, in mostly everyone's eyes is…stupid. Postmaster Meghyn and Peggy do not get along at all. Meghyn thinks Peggy is a complete idiot!

Basically, Peggy's shift is 0930 to 1830 hours with a so-called one-hour lunch break. Supervisors may stay inside all day answering phone calls, fielding customer complaints, returning customer messages, responding to email complaints (there are lots of complaints) and monitoring the retail window clerk performances. The PM supervisor also oversees the collection/dispatch mail process. Even though this supervisor experiences somewhat less stress and pressure than the AM supervisor, I would not want the PM supervisor position. Why? It's because the day seems to go by much ***slower.*** When necessary the P.M. supervisor will also go out on the street and perform street observations and document safe or unsafe driving habits on a PS Form. They may also perform a complete street audit on a troublesome carrier. This supervisor will be responsible for seeing that the post office is properly closed at end of the day and upon exiting the building will set the building alarm and lock all doors and parking lot gates.

Ms. Peggy walks onto the workroom floor and calls out, "Good morning Creeks Bend!"

"Good morning Ms. Peggy!" the employees reply.

1030: Several of the carriers have pulled down their route and have now left for the street, except Buster. At 10:30 AM, Buster yells across the floor to me at my desk "Hey Witness, I'm not going to make it in 8 hours. I'm going to need overtime." Several of the employees in his area hear him and just shake their heads. Again Buster yells, " Did you hear what I said, Witness?" By this time a couple of employees in his area have now turned around and stopped working. Now he has disrupted the floor and suddenly I have a situation on my hands. I must address it straightaway before it gets out of control. I go to him, "Buster, please quiet down." However, he only gets louderand steps closer while looking down at me. Mind you, I'm only 5'5" tall. He repeats again in a bellowing tone;

"Whatcha ya gonna do Witness? I said I need overtime to complete my assignment or else give me street assistance so I can get back in eight hours. Either way, I'm not doing all this in eight hours as you think. There's no way I can do this in the time amount you gave me."

Calmly I tell him, "Buster let's go into the office where we can talk." He challenges me, "What you gonna do write me up or send me home?" Sh*#t go ahead, send me home the hell…somebody else can carry this mess."

I knew that's what he wanted me to do but I wasn't going give in. As far as I was concerned Buster was going to carry his route today!

I steadily reiterate, "Buster please, quiet down."

By now Postmaster Meghyn walks out onto the floor and witnesses the situation. I motion for Buster to follow me into the supervisor's office.

He's steadfast, "Not without my shop steward. I want my union rep to come in with me."

Leaving him behind, I walk back to the office. Along the way, one of the employees, I think it was Rico, mumbling, "Will they ever get rid of that psycho?"

Buster gets his union rep and the three of us go into the office. Once there, Buster really goes off. *At least it's not on the open floor in front of everyone*. He likes an audience. I let him vent and when he stops. When I think he's done I ask, "Are you finished?" I tell him to return to his case, pull down his route and take it to the street. I let him know that tomorrow morning upon his arrival to work we will meet in the supervisor's office and I will conduct a PDI with him. I also give him a PS Form Carrier Request for Overtime or Assistance. He fills it out and instantaneously I deny it and sign it and give it back to him. He looked at me like I was crazy. Most managers would give into him simply because they would rather let him have his way as opposed to properly dealing with his antics.

Upon my exiting the office, postmaster Meghyn walks up to me and asked me if I gave him a PDI for disrupting the floor. I told her the conversation we had, and that I had informed him I would conduct a PDI with him tomorrow morning.

Meghyn shocked and in disbelief, "V you had him! You should have conducted PDI right then and there. You have to send these employees the right message V! Such conduct will not be tolerated, especially in my office. Suppose he calls out sick tomorrow? Heck V, if I knew I would be facing a PDI the next day I might not show up! Go grab the both of them right now and take his ass back into the office and do a PDI on him for disrupting the floor, or I will conduct a PDI on you." she threatened. The clicking of her heels echoing as she walked away.

I knew she was right. I mean, what if one of the other employees disrupted the floor? I would have conducted one on them and not just a discussion. I must be consistent. Besides, I'm sure the other employees would have expected the same as well. Stopping Willie and Buster before they had a chance to return to their route, I directed them both back into the supervisor's office for the PDI. Of course, they didn't like it and I felt stupid, mostly because of the timeliness. But right or wrong I did it anyway. Hey, I felt better afterward. Later that day, Meghyn asked me if performed the PDI on Buster. After telling her I had, she said "Thatta away V…that's my boy"!

1000 -1030: The last few carriers pull down their routes and clock out to the street. It's at this time that the postmaster may call me and the other supervisor into her office for a staff meeting.

1100 - 1330: I will spend the rest of my day fielding customer phone calls, observing carriers driving habits on the street or when necessary riding with or following a particular carrier as they perform their deliveries of mail. There are times when I will do such because an employee has challenged my instructions or because they have requested more time then what I deem necessary to deliver their assignments for that given day. Sometimes they are right and sometimes they are wrong. Therefore, they don't need the time they thought.

12:30: Lynn meets up with her boyfriend Bo and is seen getting into his van by a friend of Bo's wife. She paid this friend to spy on him. Bo's wife has been suspicious of Bo and Lynn for a while. As for the scene and what actually happened, I'll leave to your imagination.

1300: The first P.M. dispatch truck arrives at the post office to collect all accumulated outgoing mail up to this point of the day and to take it to the plant for processing. The truck also brings the Next Day/Overnight Packages. Seven of them arrive and are immediately scanned in and recorded on the daily log. Such items must be delivered or attempted delivery the same day by three o'clock P.M. or they will be considered a Failed Piece. Fortunately, three of the seven were for the P.O. Box section and so could be scanned attempted delivery, and a notice left in the customer's box indicating they have a mail item for them. All they would have to do is, upon retrieving their mail, bring the little slip and personal ID to the retail window and the window clerk would retrieve the item for them. Scanning most packages that way stops the clock on the mail piece. Now sometimes a mail piece will indicate signature is waived and in that case, the item or package is scanned delivered, and left in a secure location. But again, with a P.O. Box section item, you must still leave a notice slip in the customer's box, especially if the mail piece does not fit in the box.

1330: I clock out and leave for the day as my tour of duty, yes a military term, has ended.

1315: Ms. Peggy answers a phone call from a customer.
"Good afternoon, Creeks Bend Post Office, Peggy speaking, may I help you?"

"Could you please," asks the lady, "give me the new address for Mr.

Jones, he used to live at 222 N Main Street, Apt. 1."

"I'm sorry ma'am but we're not allowed to give such information out due to privacy," says Ms. Peggy.

"Yes, I understand but I was hoping I could find out where he had moved, I wanted to send him an invitation to a party I'm hosting later this month."

"Again ma'am," says Peggy, "I can not give you that information, I'm so sorry but you'll have to locate him some other way, okay?"

"Well, okay, I guess you're not going to help me," says the lady.

"I'm sorry ma'am," responded Ms. Peggy.

"Oh, you're a miserable person," quips the lady to Peggy, and disconnects.

1320: Phone rings: "Good afternoon, Creeks Bend Post Office, Ms. Peggy speaking may I help you?"

"Well, I don't know if you can help me…hell, I'm just trying to help you," stated the customer.

"Oh, okay sounds great! So sir, how can you help us today," asked Ms. Peggy?

"Okay, well it goes like this. Today at about twelve thirty, I saw one of your postal trucks pull up behind this old abandoned building across the street from our apartment complex. I thought it looked funny cause I ain't never seen one of your trucks over there before and everything like that, and I know no mail gets delivered there. So I said to myself, 'Self, somethin' looks like it's gettin ready to go down over there.' So I just continued to watch and then the mail lady got out of her truck and got into this custom built like van that was parked right next to her post office truck. Now I knew dat wasn't right, so I just kept lookin to see what was goin on, ya know what I'm sayin? And so after a few minutes, I saw what looked like them climbing into the back of the van. So then I'm thinking to myself look like somebody gettin ready to get busy."

"WHAT?!" shouted Ms. Peggy.

"Yeah, right?! Like I mean they were in the van for about forty-five minutes."

"What?! You're kidding me," said Ms. Peggy.

"No, no way, I'm for real! I think they were having sex. Listen I ain't trying to get nobody in trouble and everything like that there but I just thought ya'llshould know what I saw."

"Do you remember what time it was, sir?"

"Yeah, of course I do! Like I already said, it was about twelve-thirty." "Do you recall what the number on the postal truck was sir," asked Ms. Peggy?

"Ummm, it was somethin' like, umm. Well, no, I don't actually remember all the numbers but I do know that it ended like in 3777."

"Are you sure those were the numbers sirs?"

"I know that for a fact because that's my lucky lotto number. You know like it's a combination of lucky three sevens...3777!"

"Oh, really, so you're very sure?"

"Shoot, heck yeah…all the way I'm sure!"

"Well, sir, I really appreciate your call and for letting us know. Listen, Mr.-what did you say your name was?"

"Oh, no way…sh*#t, I ain't given up my name."

"Well, would you be willing to give us a written statement of what you just told me or what you saw? Or perhaps I myself could come out and meet you and talk with you," said Ms. Peggy.

"Nah, that's alright. You know like they say, lady, 'everything is everything.'"

And the phone went dead.

1325: Ms. Peggy documented the call on her notepad. She then sent an email to Meghyn detailing the phone conversation.

1327: Meghyn pages Peggy. "Peggy intercom ten please, Peggy intercom ten."

Peggy rolled her eyes and then proceeded to dial Meghyn's extension.

"Peggy!"

"Yes, Meghyn?"

"Are you serious? You've got to be kidding me?"

"No Meghyn. I just got off the phone with the gentleman and he appeared to be serious to me!"

"Well, did he say he was willing to give us a statement?"
"No. He basically said that he didn't want to get involved like that."

"Yeah, right…no one ever wants to get involved. Well, I want you to do a PDI with Lynn as soon as she returns to the post office."

"Ok, I will Meghyn."

1500: Phone rings: "Good afternoon and thank you for calling the Creeks Bend Post Office, Ms. Peggy speaking may I help you?"

(It's an emergency call from the mail carrier, Old Man)

"Hello, Ms. Peggy this Old Man calling."

"Old Man? Uh oh! What's wrong Mr. Old Man, are you okay?"

"I'm sorry Ms. Peggy but I just can't continue on today so I gonna bring my route back. I can't make any further today."

"Now Old Man what's wrong?"

"Ms. Peggy my hands hurt terribly and my arms and shoulders are killing me. I can't even grab the mail now. It's the Rheumatoid arthritis…been bothering me all morning. I thought I could make it through the day but I just can't. I fell badly about this but I gotta come back…you're gonna have to get someone else to finish my route. I'm so sorry…"
"Oh, my goodness Mr. Old Man, about how much of your route is left?"

"I have about three and half hours yet to be done."

"What?! Three and a half hours? Mr. Old Man what have you doing out there? It's nearly two o'clock PM! You've already been out there for four hours! Come on Old Man, you can't do this to me! Where am I gonna find somebody to finish your route? The carriers are already calling saying they're gonna be late getting back! Now Old Man, you know your route's not that big that you should have that much time left!"

"Well, Ms. Peggy, I hear what you're saying but I just can't go on any longer. And I don't know if I'll even be in tomorrow. I'll be back to the office in about ten minutes."

"Well, Old Man how about if I just call someone, and have them meet you out there and take some of your route off of you?"

"No, Ms. Peggy! I can't make it! Heck, the way my hands feel and are hurting, I hope I can safely drive back to the office."

"Old Man, you really need to retire!"

"Now Ms. Peggy you know that was totally uncalled for…not nice at all. As many years as I have given to this place…you people... listen I'm ending this phone call…gotta go…I'm on my way back now. I'll see you when I get back there. Bye!"

"But but Old Man…hello…Old Man…hello?"

*Oh, brother, these carriers can really have some issues. And now his issues have become my issues. What am I gonna do now?*said

Ms. Peggy to herself.

Peggy began walking toward Postmaster Meghyn's office to get some advice. But as soon as Meghyn saw her approaching she put up her hand as if to say STOP and halted Peggy in her steps and said to Ms. Peggy… "Peggy, please shut my door I'm busy right now. It will have to wait a moment." As usual, Peggy dropped her head, hands at her sides, grabbed a chair and waited outside of Meghyn's office until she finished her phone conversation with her daughter.

Meghyn was involved in a heated discussion with her just turned seventeen-year-old daughter who wants to go out tonight; a school night of all days, with a couple of her friends. From what I heard there was a bowling party being hosted by one her girlfriend's parents at the local bowling lane. The problem is Meghyn had grounded her daughter for two weeks on account of unsatisfactory grades and poor attendance at school. From what I hear, Meghyn's daughter is just like Meghyn when it comes to temper, fight and will. But trust me, Meghyn is the head honcho here and at home and not only does she win battles, she wins wars!

Well, just as Ms. Peggy got ready to stand up and walk away she heard Meghyn slam the phone down, walk toward the closed door of her office, high heels clicking, and opened the door. Sarcastically, she smiles at Peggy and asks… "What's up Peggy?" Peggy began informing her about the conversation she had with Old Man and asked Meghyn what she should do about it. In her intolerant way,

Meghyn shook her head and said, "Peggy you have been a supervisor here for four years now…you should know how to handle these matters."

"I know Meghyn I'm just a little rattled by the conversation I just had with Old Man and the other customer calls. It's really caught me off-guard. I'm sorry I will work it out. I'm so sorry to bother you Meghyn."

Both simply walk away from each other, seemingly disgusted with one another. Meghyn more so disgusted then Peggy. As Meghyn walked away from Peggy she mumbled to herself, *She is worthless… boy, I regret the day I hired her.* Meghyn then picked up her purse and other items, locked her door and left for the day.

Old Man arrived back to the office with mail still yet to be delivered. He slowly and painfully dismounted from out of the truck and handed Ms. Peggy the truck keys.

"I'm sorry Ms. Peggy but I can't go on any further I got to get to my doctor I'm really hurting. My hands and neck are killing me."

"Old Man," replied Peggy, "when are you going to retire? Heck, you're killing me! You can't just keep going on like this. I can't keep having you bringing back undelivered mail like this. Especially this much at this time of the day!"

"Yeah, yeah yeah, I know Ms. Peggy. I heard what you said before."

"Well, Old Man can you at least split the mail up into four forty-five minute pieces so I can get carriers to deliver it when they get back? I need to have them when they get back to immediately go back out again. I can't have them wasting time figuring out how to split up all this mail you brought back."

"I'm sorry Ms. Peggy, I can't." he implored. "I got to get out of here now! I'm really hurting."

"But Old Man what am I going to do? I don't know your route," entreated Peggy. "I don't have time to figure this out! I have no idea how to split up your route."

"Ms. Peggy," Old Man apologetically stated, "I'm sorry, I can't help you…I gotta go!"

1530: Chip had taken his ten-minute street break to gather up his undelivered mis-sequenced and mis-sent mail, and called his daughter Carly from his cell phone.

Carly's phone rang barely one time as she quickly answered it. "Hey, dad how was work today?"

"Oh, just another routine day honey. Only it's a day that is nearing the end of my mailman days. Ya know, Carly, it feels really weird."

Chip stated.

1625: Some of the carriers begin returning back to the office upon completing their delivery duties. Lynn returns back to the post office as well. She's all smiley faced and perky as she pulled her postal delivery truck into her route's parking slot. Guess who was waiting in the parking lot? Yup…it was Bo's wife, Renalda, and oh brother she looked sorely ***LIVID***, to say the least. Well, as soon as Lynn stepped out of her postal truck, out of nowhere appeared Renalda stepping right into Lynn's path. She began hollering and screaming at Lynn calling her all kinds of names and using some pretty foul phrases as one might have expected considering the circumstance. One can only imagine what was actually said. From what I heard, Lynn also must have called Renalda a name or two because one of the employees standing nearby quickly grabbed Renalda as she was getting ready to haul off and take a swing at Lynn. Lynn had supposedly referred to Renalda as a "low life, pitiful, drunk, alcoholic."

I had heard, through the "grapevine" that Renalda had threatened Lynn and had warned her to stay away from her husband Bo, or she would be sorry. Renalda, as the story went, told Lynn that she was "nothing more than a polluted, self-centered whore, who preyed on married men."

Lynn, I'm sure, was quite embarrassed as there were other employees in the parking lot who had witnessed the event.

Although Renalda never touched Lynn physically, Lynn apparently cowered under the onslaught of words and yelling. Needless to say, she was quite shaken. There had been a rumor circulating that Renalda had grabbed and pulled Lynn's hair. In the end, that turned out to be just a rumor. That rumor was perpetuated by, of course, two male employees who witnessed the incident and thought the whole event was entertaining; Reds and Marlon. Scenes like this were right down their alley. Those guys would eat this up.

Thank God for Lynn's sake, Renalda, at least this time was not that intoxicated. Even though she had verbally attacked Lynn, she did not physically touch or harm her. She came pretty close to doing so though. It seems Renalda was stable minded enough to maintain her boundaries while on postal property. I know Renalda, given the chance, would have ripped Lynn apart. Lynn's too much of a princess to be a fighter. Had Renalda harmed Lynn she would have been in serious trouble as it's a Federal crime to physically assault a postal employee.

1645: Before clocking out at the time clock Ms. Peggy approached Lynn to ask if she wanted to file a harassment charge against Chip's wife Renalda.

Without hesitation, Lynn quickly sputtered, "NO!" Clocking out she added "I won't be in to work tomorrow…after today there's NO WAY I'm coming in tomorrow. I have never felt so humiliated and embarrassed. I don't know why this had to happen to me!"

Hmmm, poor little Lynn such an innocent human being, totally misunderstood and the victim once again…mumbled Ms. Peggy to herself.

"Hey, Ms. Lynn wait! I need you to step into the office. I need to ask you some questions about a phone call I received this afternoon from one of the customers on your route."

"What Ms. Peggy? I've already clocked out and you want me to clock back in so you can take me into the office and question me? Yeah, right! Well, that ain't happening today Ms. Peggy. Besides, I want representation and there's no union representative here."

"Well, then we will just have to do it tomorrow."

"Yeah, right! Listen, Ms. Peggy, the way I feel right now I most likely won't be in tomorrow. So I'm letting you know now…I will not be in!"

"Well, Ms. Lynn, you know the procedure, you will have to call the eight hundred number in the morning to let them know of your absence. And then please call here afterward to let Mr. V know. Okay?"

Without missing a beat, Lynn abruptly pressed, "Ms. Peggy I'm telling you right now that I will not be in tomorrow…you can leave a note for Mr. V saying so."

"Well, Ms. Lynn," continued Ms. Peggy, "You will be charged AWOL then."

"Whatever Ms. Peggy, whatever," Lynn shrugged off the warning as she walked out the door.

Several other employees were standing by and witnessed the conversation between Ms. Peggy and Lynn. One of them said, with a smile, "Hey Ms. Peggy, just like Forrest Gump said in the movie. 'Life is like a box of chocolates…you never know what you're gonna get.'"

Chip was also standing by and had witnessed the conversation. He threw his hands up in the air and said, "Only in the post office…only in the post office"!

"You got that right Chip, you certainly got that right." Ms. Peggy mused, letting her words trail offas she walked back to the supervisor's desk to document the conversation she had with Lynn.

1700: By now the rest of the carriers had returned back to the post office. Of course, they already knew what went down between Lynn and Renalda. The incident would be the main topic of discussion on the workroom floor tomorrow when the employees clock in. As soon as there is action in the office the employees get on their cell phones and begin calling one another. It's like whisper down the lane. One calls one and on it goes

1701: Spice went outside to collect the mail that postal patrons had deposited into the blue collection boxes located outside in the postal parking lot. She would also scan the collection box label with a scanning device and once back inside would then place the scanning device on the scanner cradle for the information to be downloaded. By properly scanning and placing the gadget into the cradle, District would be notified and informed that the collection mailbox had been successfully emptied of the mail that was put into it and that the box was properly scanned. If not, the scanning clerk or even the supervisor would have to go back outside and rescan the box.

Technically, the official labeled scanning time is five o'clock or, in postal time, 1700 hours. However, Spice, or whoever is assigned to the duty, would wait until one or two minutes past five o'clock before actually scanning the label in the mailbox. If she scans the label too soon it would count as a failure and would need to be rescanned. No supervisor, I repeat, *NO supervisor* can leave the post office until all collection mailboxes have been scanned and emptied of their mail, and verified by District personnel.

1710: All of the day's collection mail brought back carriers and any retrieved from outside since the last dispatch truck would now be separated and containerized according to mail size, letters, large envelopes and metered mail or non-stamped mail.

1730: The last dispatch truck departs from the loading dock and leaves the post office en route to the plant to be processed.

1800: Well, after another eventful postal day, and upon finishing the PM paperwork Ms. Peggy finally clocked out, set the alarm, and exited the building. The work day was officially over. Stepping into her car to go pick up her two children at her sister's house. Peggy and her husband, at this point, were separated so Peggy's sister would usually pick the two children up after school and take them home with her until Peggy got off work.

After work Chip and his daughter Carly met up at about seven o'clock p.m. and went to the tuxedo shop for Chip to be fitted for the tuxedo that he would wear for her wedding. Her wedding colors were white, of course, and blue. This was out of respect for Chip's U.S. Marine military background that his daughter Carly decided to choose a shade of blue as her wedding color. She really admired her father and it was obvious to everyone who knew them. There was nothing she couldn't talk about to him. He had always provided her an open platform on which she could speak about anything.

After finishing up at the tuxedo store they went out for dinner to a local French-Japanese restaurant called Shangri-La. He even bought her a bottle of her favorite wine; Woodbridge, a soft white wine. The evening weather was a balmy, seventy degrees out so they decided to eat dinner outside on the restaurant's rooftop deck. There they discussed the final details of her wedding. Being so detail oriented, Chip had been a big help in assisting Carly with the planning of her wedding. They ate their appetizers, entrée, dessert, and finished things off with an after dinner cordial.

It was at this time that Carly asked her father for the first time since her mother's passing. "Dad, I know mom was cremated and there was no viewing or service for her. Heck, I guess that's what she wanted. But is that what you wanted? I mean, would you have done things differently if it had been up to you? Would you have had a viewing for her or even some type of service like a memorial service or something like that?"

"Well, you know Carly, yes that was your mother's request, but to be quite honest I wish we had chosen, I wish I had chosen to have a memorial service, you know? Some type of gathering. You know like a time for people to share their thoughts, a time to share memories. A time for all who knew her to come together and to acknowledge her life. You know, a time to express our feelings. We could have played her favorite songs. Sure it would have been sad but I think it's healing.I think it's comforting. We humans are so ceremonial and I think it's important to come together as a community to acknowledge that a life had been lived. To acknowledge that a person is special and that they have touched our lives is so important. I mean, when someone passes away we become their witnesses. We bear testimony that their life was lived, that their life meant something, that their life had meaning. We need to pause and take the time to embrace one another and find comfort. * I wish I had done that with your mother's services."

"Oh, dad, I didn't mean to make you feel bad or guilty," said Carly.

"Oh, that's ok honey, you didn't. But hey, if something was ever to happen to me and I pass away, please have a gathering for me, and then bury me with my full military honors. I earned it, okay?"

Carly said to her father… "Dad, let's not think about that. I don't know what I would do without you. I couldn't bear to lose you, especially since mom's gone." Grabbing her father's hand, "Promise me, dad."

"Promise you what honey?"

"Promise me that you will never leave me."

"Oh, Carly sweetheart stop it."

"No dad, I'm serious. Promise me that you won't leave me like mom did."

There was a pause, and then as Chip was about to reply, Carly quickly apologized to him and said, "Oh, dad, I'm so sorry. I didn't mean to say that. I mean, I didn't mean to say it like that. I know mom didn't to choose to leave me or us…it just hurts. It hurts me that I won't have her here on my wedding day. And even to see you retire. I mean you've worked so hard and long to be able to retire and to share that time together with her and then she dies and just like that the dream is gone. It's just not fair…life's not fair."

"I know Carly. I get down and a bit angry at times myself. And you're right Carly, life isn't fair. But no matter what you have to trust God. Anyway young lady, don't you worry, I'm not going anywhere soon. Besides, I wouldn't miss your wedding day for anything in the world. Heck, you're all I have now."

The waiter came back with the dinner bill. Chip began to reach into his pocket but Carly quickly stopped him. I got this one dad! You are going to need all the money you can find to pay for my wedding tab!" as she stood up with a huge grin on her face.

"Yeah, honey, how right you are…" replied Chip.

Of course, Carly was joking, for she knew her dad had been saving up for years for this beautiful moment in her life.

CHAPTER TWO

DAY TWO, Thursday

0300: My alarm clock goes off and I begin my daily routine.

0350: Bitsy pulls up to the chained lock gate, getting out of her car to unlock it. As she slowly pushed the right gate open, she stops, looks into the faintly lit parking lot and notices something unusual.

"What in the world…a peacock? Is that a…peacock? Oh, my God, it really is a
Peacock! How in the world did it get in here?" wondered Bitsy.

0353: Pudgy then pulls into the parking lot. She swiftly stopped, and slowly leaning forward over the steering wheel in disbelief of what she was seeing.

"Oh, my word, that's a BIG bird! Oh, my goodness, it's a peacock!"

Bitsy, seeing Pudgy slowly pulling up to the post office, lifts both of her arms up into the air as if to check they were seeing the same thing.

Pudgy parks her SUV in her usual spot and hurries into the building where Bitsy is waiting, holding the door open for her.

0400: They both swipe their time badges through the time clock and then proceed to cautiously go back outside to take another look at the peacock.

Peeping around the corner to see where the Peacock was, they are spooked by a loud screech and dashed back into the building screaming.

0410: The first transportation truck arrives with the first trip mail. Of course, both Pudgy and Bitsy are intimidated by the peacock outside and are afraid to go out on the dock to help unload the truck. The driver ends up unloading the mail off the truck by himself. Eventually, they both go out to help him once they feel that it's safe to do so.

0415: I pull into the postal parking lot, back up my car and say my prayer.

0420: I walk into the building along with Samantha. It's her scheduled day off, giving her time and a half pay, making her very happy. Samantha loves the overtime. The both of us, Samantha first, swipe our employee time badges and clock in consecutively. Samantha then walks into the ladies room. Actually, all employees, according to the postal manual, are supposed to go into the locker room first and take care of their personal business before clocking in, that way they are ready for duty once clocking in. Some do, some don't.

Bitsy, as is her usual custom approaches me and without even saying good morning begins to unload on me.

"Mr. V, I have bad news and I have some…bad news. Which do you want first," she asked with a grin on her face.

I just looked at her with my usual morning face, and she proceeded to inform me that CeeDee called out sick but that she would try to be in tomorrow. CeeDee claimed that she was feeling dizzy and weak, which are her usual symptoms and reason for calling out. I just shake my head in disgust and walk away.

She went on to say, "Secondly Mr. V, we just finished spreading the super market circulars. Boy did they take a long time. You know the construction work being done to the new loading dock, and the makeshift lift that we have to use is really causing problems. It slows down the process of unloading the truck. Bitsy was nearly hurt when several of the APCs tumbled over and ended up coming off the truck. When that happened all of the mail fell out of the APCs. What a mess Mr. V!"

"Yea, and the APCs that fell over," said Bitsy, "contained mail that had already been carrier routed but now have to be hand sorted at the case. So now it's going take us longer to sort the mail because it's all out of order now."

Great, I said to myself, "So now the carriers will be delayed in getting out to the street on time. If it's not one thing it's another!"

"Yeah, and to top it all off, there's a peacock outside in the parking lot."

"What…a peacock?"

"Yup, a peacock! Go outside and take a look why don't you."

"No thanks, I'll take you at your word."

"What a way to start the morning, huh Mr.?" groaned Pudgy. "Gee whiz, had I known it was going to be like this I would have called out sick and stayed home too." she saidsmiling.

Bitsy whispered to Samantha, "Yeah, I wish she had. It seems like we get things done a lot faster when she's not around."

Pudgy said to me later, "Mr. V, you should really have someone from safety come out here and take a look at this dock situation because in my opinion, that's a safety hazard. In fact, I think I will write up a safety complaint form and give it to you or Meghyn."

"Yeah, right, this whole place is a safety hazard." I say aloud as I walk away.

"Uh oh, I guess Mr. V's not in a good mood." said Bitsy.

I walk over to the supervisor desk, put down my bottle of tea, and begin my tour around the office for inspection. Once finished, I return to the desk and start my daily routine on the computer.

0530: Chip's phone rings. It's Carly giving her father Chip his daily good morning call. The conversation goes on as usual and ending in "I love you…talk to you later."

0558: Mason walks through the door, standing in the middle of the workroom floor. His hands on his hips in their usual way, he glared at us all. He does this for two minutes and then clocks in at 0600 hours. Inspector gadget is officially here and on the clock. He then walked over to me and motioned, "Oooutsiiide oooutsiiide peeeacock peeeacock."

"Yes, I know Mason, I know there's a peacock outside."

"Nooo good nooo good…call call." continued Mason.

"Yes, Mason, we are taking care of it." satisified, he walked away.

0620: Telephone rings. I pause for a moment, take a breath and then answer.

"Good morning, Creeks Bend Post Office, Mr. V speaking may I help you?"

"Good morning, this is Tom DuPaulo the plant manager."

"Oh, good morning sir, I thought you might have been another employee calling out sick or something." I say to him relieved.

"No, not quite," said the manager, "I'm calling to inform you that the next truck is going to be late. Unfortunately, it contains parcels that were mis-sent to another office. The truck broke down on its way to that office and it took about forty minutes to get it up and running again. So it will be a good forty to forty-five minutes to an hour late getting to you. And yes I know that this will delay your carriers leave time to the street."

"Yes, it will," I replied. "About how many parcels will be on the truck?" I asked.

"Well, think it will contain two full skids of parcels that will have to be broken down, sorted and taken out to the street for delivery today by the carriers. I realize that these parcels will arrive past the mail distribution cut off time but they must, I repeat must go out today. No package can be left behind. They are time sensitive packages and must be either delivered or attempted delivery to the homes today."

"Oh, boy, alright…okay, we'll make sure they go out today."

"Yes, please do," said the plant manager, "it is imperative that we adhere to the sender's request. We can't afford to lose their business. They are a major mailer and as you know, due to the internet, the parcel business is the fastest growing segment of our business and we must do everything possible to keep it going in that direction."

"Yes, sir I understand, we'll get them out today!"

"Oh, and what's your name again?" asked the manager.

"My name is Mr. V, I'm the morning supervisor."

"Ok, Mr. V, thank you for your compliance. Please email me when the skids arrive and the sorting of them has been completed. So long and have a good day."

"So long, sir," I replied as I thought to myself, *Yeah right, you have a good day too.*

So now this means that the carriers will be an extra hour late getting out to the street. On top of that, the letters that will now have to be manually sorted. Why didn't the plant get these skids of parcels out to us yesterday afternoon? We always get a shipment in the afternoon. Did they just arrive this morning? You can count on the plant to screw up an operation. Uhhh…will I EVER get out of this place? I say to myself.

Today the carriers have the super market circulars that are scheduled to go out on Thursdays and you know that's a struggle in itself. Trying to get the carriers, especially the walkers back on time with the Super Market circulars. And on top of that, the late arriving parcels, and hand sorted letters? I can hear the carriers now, 'It's going to take longer Mr. V because now we have to go to every house because of the circulars. And with the extra volume of parcels, there's no way we're going to able to make it back in time to make the last dispatch truck.'

We'll just have to send a carrier, or possibly even Peggy, to the plant tonight with the late returning carrier's outgoing mail. Nobody likes making that trip! Uhhh, how I hate this job, if it's not one thing it's another! What else is going happen, I exclaim? MAN, I can't WAIT 'til I can retire!

0650: Telephone rings several times. I was slow answering it. Samantha picked up the phone and said, "Good morning, Creeks Bend Post Office Samantha speaking, may I help you?"

"Samantha, this is Lynn, is Mr. V there?"

"Yes, he is. Just a moment Lynn, let me get him for you. Hey, Mr. V, it's for you…it's Lynn," as she hands me the phone biting her nails.

Having been informed of the situation, I slowly take the phone and answered, "Y-yyes Lynn"?

"Hey, I told Ms. Peggy yesterday that I would not be in today so I'm calling out sick and I won't be in."

"And why not?" I probed.

"Mr. V, I don't feel well and I will not be in today."

"Well, do you think you will be in tomorrow?" I asked.

"At this point, I'm not sure, maybe I will maybe I won't. I'm just so embarrassed and humiliated."

Humiliated, I thought to myself. She ought to feel ashamed. I mean, she was runnin' with another woman's husband and she got busted... and she feels humiliated?

"Alright, Lynn, we'll see you tomorrow."

Without saying anything more, she hung up.

Well, there goes any plans I had for getting the carriers back on time today. What else is going to happen? I then said to myself, V, don't ask!

0650 – 0700: I had the distribution clerks performing other work and taking the super market flyers around to the routes while waiting for the truck to arrive with the mail.

Marlon showed up early, I take advantage of it, instructing him to clock in and start casing up the mail on Lynn's route as she had called out sick and would not be in.

Meghyn walked out of her office and as usual, gives her greeting. "Good Morning V!"

"Good morning Meghyn." I said in a low voice and with my head down.

"What's wrong?" she asked

I brief her on the situation telling her about the sick call, the super market flyers, and the packages that will be arriving late from the plant.

"WHAT…why…what packages…how many?! When are they going to arrive? Who called? I'm sorry V, I haven't given you a chance to answer any of my questions have I?"

I just looked at her and shook my head as if to say no. I inhaled before answering her. "The plant manager called about an hour ago. Apparently, the packages were mis-sent to another office so they had to send out a truck to retrieve them and get them to us. However, while the truck was in transit it broke down."

"Do you know how many packages we're going to receive?" she asked.

"He said two skids."

"Two skids?"

"Yup, two skids!"

"That's approximately three hundred parcels which equates to about twenty extra parcels per route. That could equate to at least an extra twenty to thirty minutes of street time per route." she said.

"Yeah, I know, especially with the circulars and carriers having to carry a section of another route."

"WHAT? We'll have carriers out past the last dispatch truck! They won't make it back in time. This is unacceptable, Meghyn said in frustration. You know V we shoot ourselves in the foot every time. Well, if the parcels don't get here in time we'll just have to curtail them until tomorrow. They'll just have to wait until tomorrow."

"I don't think so Meghyn…they're all priority packages. They gotta go out today!"

"If that's not Murphy's Law…*whatever can go wrong will go wrong.* You can count on the plant for screwing up the day! That's a bunch of bull crap...all they care about is getting the mail out of their hands."

"Yeah, right, and that's not all of it."
"Why, what do you mean?" Meghyn asked.

"Well, several of the APCs of carrier routed letters fell over while unloading the truck. Fortunately, some of the trays stayed in tack, but many others fell out of order. So they will have to be hand sorted at the clerk case. And, there's a peacock out in the parking lot."

"WHAT, a peacock?"

"Yup, a peacock."

"Do you know how it got here or where it come from?"

"Yeah, I think it came through the mail on the first transportation truck."

"Oh, come on V, don't play with me."

"I don't know how it got here Meghyn. Besides, my job is supervising the clerks and the carriers, not peacocks."

Meghyn, threw up her hands, walked away and proceeded to mail distribution area. She grabbed a few trays of letters and started putting the letters back in order. She instructed one of the carriers to clock in and do the same. Now I knew that would be a grievance; management performing craft work. Sure enough, Pudgy picked up a notepad and started taking notes of what Meghyn was doing and notated the time. She would, later that day, ask for union time to write up her grievance. Of course, Meghyn could care less. She would rather pay out grievance money than to have the carriers standing around waiting for the mail to be processed.

0715: Marlon, as he is casing mail at Lynn's case, hears Buster walk through the door as he enters the post office. Marlon, seeing Buster, immediately blurts out "Oh, look who it is…if it isn't Mr. Big Mouth himself!"

"Yeah, well, how you supposed to see me, lover boy? You posta be facing the case and casing up that mail." responded Buster. "You keep it up and you'll be crusin for a bruisin!"

As Buster, reeking of marijuana, proceeds to the men's room, Chip chimed in by singing Phil Collins's song,"*Oh, think twice, it's just another day for you and me in paradise."*

"Oh, yeah good one Chippie boy." said Marlon.

"Hey, Chip, how many more swipes at the clock do you have?" asked Reds.

"Eight more guys, eight more swipes at the clock and then I'm outta here." he responded.

0730: The carriers clocked into work and proceeded to go outside to perform their daily routine of inspecting their postal vehicles. Before they step outside, even though signs were posted, I let them know peacock had been spotted outside in the parking lot, but it is safe for them to go outside. I notice Zakar is late.

As everyone swiped in and walked outside to inspect their trucks they began talking about yesterday's altercation involving Lynn and the woman in the postal parking lot. News like that spreads around the post office at the speed of light. I'm sure the neighboring post office employees had heard about it before they even made it home last night. Hey, that's what happens! People get on their phones and begin calling around to their buddies. Buster, the marijuana odor still strong, exited the men's room, briskly walking over to the time clock and swiped his timecard. He asked: "Where's the little hussy at"? , referencing Lynn.

"What? Who are you talking about Buster?" calmly asked Pudgy, shaking her head and shrugging her shoulders, as she and Samantha were standing nearby.

"Oh, don't give me that…you know damn well who I'm talkin' about! The hussy is out there posta be delivering mail but instead she's out there in some van screwin'. Oh, well I hope at least she was on her lunch break!"

Buster then chuckled and proceeded to walk outside to inspect his vehicle. Pudgy looked over at Samantha and said, "Oh, boy here we go. It's gonna be an interesting morning." Samantha responded by saying, "Yup I'm afraid you're right Pudgy. You know how this place is, there's no mercy around here."
"Yeah, I guess you're right, everyone's talking about it. Heck, by the time we all got home last night we all probably had heard every little detail," replied Samantha.

0735: Carriers return back in from their vehicle inspections and report to their cases. There were no incidents or sightings of the peacock. So that was a relief. I announce over the intercom about the open route due to the sick call and that they will be carrying their own routes as well as a portion of another route. I disclose information about the situation regarding the packages that will be arriving late. Lastly, I share with them that I would be coming around with their daily instructions in a few minutes.

0740: First I went to Old Man and instructed him on his assignment. Then to Chip. Chip's instructions were, that he would be carrying one hour's worth of work on Lynn's route as I had to split it up because of her calling out sick.

"Man this place is killing me." said Chip. "But okay, it's just going to be another long day but we'll get it done." he said wit ha smile.

"Thanks, Chip." I responded, "Thanks for your cooperation. I'm sure going to miss you man. If I had ten carriers like you this office would not need a supervisor."

"No problem Mr. V, and thanks for the compliment."

Reds was to carry forty-five minutes of Lynn's route and that he should be back to the office by five o'clock PM. Per the usual, he began to question my authority.

"I don't know what numbers you're looking at, but I'm barely going to make five o'clock on my own route. You'll be lucky if I make it back by six! I probably won't make the last dispatch truck for that matter."

"Look Reds, I responded, "You have eight hours' worth of work on your route plus an additional forty-five minutes on Lynn's."

"Listen Mr. V," sassed Reds, "First of all, your numbers are based on unsubstantiated data and therefore are wrong. Secondly, you're giving me forty-five minutes of street delivery, not including the eight minutes of travel time each way. Now any intelligent manager would know that that assignment really equates to over an hour's worth of work. Not to mention the fact that I have the super market flyers today. PLUS I'm leaving a half hour later than my posted schedule leave time because you people are making us wait for the packages. And who knows how many packages I'm gonna receive on that truck?"

"Well, we're just going to have to curtail the super markets until tomorrow." I responded.

"Well, I tell you what, it's gonna take more than curtailing the super markets!" said Reds. "Listen Mr. V, I'm not trying to be difficult, but at the end of the day it is what it is!"

"We will see once all the mail has arrived." I move on to the next carrier, Buster. *Oh, boy here we go again,* I thought to myself.

"Good morning Buster and how are you doing this morning?"

"Good morning? What's so good about it, huh Witness? It was fine until you showed up…in fact, my day was perfect until I got to this place."

"Yeah, that's because he was probably getting high on his way to work." mumbled Old Man.

"Yeah!"

"Well, Buster…"

"WELL Buster, WELL Buster? How you know I'm well, Witness? What, you some doctor now or something…how you know how I feel? You gonna come to me talking about some well Buster."

"Yeah, **WELL** sounds like a deep subject." laughed Marlon.

"Ha ha ha, real funny, sounds like a deep subject," echoed Buster to Marlon sarcastically voice. "I guess you think that now qualifies you for being some kinda psychologist, huh little man! You supervisors crack me up, gonna try to tell me how to do my job. How are you gonna give me orders? You ain't casing and carrying this mail. You just sittin' inside all day on your ass looking at some fudged up numbers thinkin' you da boss. Maybe if you ASKED me to do my job I might do it. But you ain't gonna get nowhere with me by giving me some orders like you're the boss."

"Well, he is the supervisor and I think that translates into the boss." said Chip. "Actually the word supervisor means overseer or to oversee and operation."

"Oh, now listen to Mister Goodie Two Shoes! There he goes always supporting management."

After that brief, heated, exchange of words, Buster looked at me and said, "So what Witness, Mister Overseer Supervisor…are you gonna give me my instructions now or do I have to shake it out of you?"

"Alright Buster…"

Alright? Alright my eye! Ain't nothing alright this morning, including what you're about to say to me. I knew I should've stayed home! Better yet, I wish you had stayed home Witness!"

"Yeah, we wish you had stayed home too Buster," said Oliver!

"Yeah!"

"I don't know about that Buster," responded Old Man. "Who would you rather have supervising the floor, Mr. V or the Queen Bee?"

"Yeah, you got that right…tell him Old Man!" replied Willie.

"Yeah, not the Queen Bee, her sting is much worse, and she screws up everything!"

I started at him for a moment and continued to give him his daily instructions. As was his typical response he stared down at me, "Yeah, right whatever Witness." He turned away from me and started casing his mail again. I then said to him, "I will be back around later Buster, okay?"

"Yeah, okay Witness, whatever, everything is everything…I'm gonna go to the men's room."

"What's the matter Buster, you sick again?" asked Rico.

"No, I'm not sick, my stomach is sick." shot back Buster.

"Hehe he…I guess Mr. Buster didn't like what Mr. V said to him." said Oliver as he guffawed. He sounded like the character Horshak from the old TV show *Welcome Back Kotter.*

Chip looked at me and just shook his head, "That Buster sure has a way with words doesn't he?"
I nodded my head yes manner and softly chuckled.

0750: Zakar reports late to work again.

0755: Buster forcefully entered the men's restroom.

Gino and Habib also went into the men's room and are carrying on a conversation about the customer's on Habib's route.

"Habib," said Gino, "Doesn't it seem like the postmaster has been on your case a lot lately?"

"Yeah, yeah," he responded. "It's like I can't do anything right Gino! And I don't think the customers on my route like me. They are always calling here with complaints."

"Yeah, I know, and besides that, I don't think Meghyn likes us," said Gino. "We rural carriers have always been treated like stepchildren in the post office. Heck, we're the most productive force in the post office. Yet management is constantly looking for ways to cut our pay. In my opinion, the city carriers are one of the reasons why the post office is losing money. Think about it, I have a route that has over seven hundred and seventy stops. My average daily mail volume is approximately fifteen feet of mail, which includes about four feet of flats and about eleven feet of letters. Not to mention the packages I deliver. Now I can case up all of that mail in about two and half hours, depending on the thickness of the mail. I then can deliver that mail in about four hours. It takes me about six and a half to seven hours to get my work done. Now give a city carrier that same volume of work and it will take them about nine and a half to ten hours. That's two and a half to three hours longer than I would take. And I know you know why?"

"Yeah! They get paid by the hour." replied Habib.

"Yes, exactly! They get paid by the hour. And so their incentive is to stretch the job out because the longer they take the more money they make. There's no reward in them getting the work done sooner! Our routes, the RD routes, are evaluated. So it behooves us to get the job done faster. If my route is fairly evaluated to take eight hours and I only take six and a half to seven hours to complete it then I'm still gonna get paid my evaluation. Heck, I usually get home three to four hours before these guys do. If the post office wants to save money they should have all the routes on the evaluated system. I mean I know it's not the answer to solving all the problems the post office has but it's surely a step in the right direction."

"Well, that's not going to happen because the city carrier union would never agree to that." replied Habib.

"I know! It's because their union members would lose a bunch of money if they no longer got paid per hour. Many of the city carriers make sixtyfive to seventy grand or more a year. Heck, some have even boasted about making nearly a hundred grand. Contrast that with a rural carrier who maybe makes fortythree to fiftyfive thousand a year. And you know every year, at least twice a year, upper management looks for ways to cut rural carrier salaries by doing those one to two week long inspections. Well, we may make less money but at least we get home earlier and get thus get to spend more time with our families or whatever we like to do."

"Yeah, yeah," replied Habib. "I couldn't stay here at work all day like some of these people do."

Out of the blue, Buster shouts out from one of the stalls, "I wish you guys would shut up. I can't hear myself go. I don't just like feeling myself going I also need to hear myself going."

"Sorry Buster, we didn't realize it meant that much to you."

"Yeah, right, hahaha." clucked Buster.

"Well, Habib I guess we better let Buster go in peace."

As Gino and Habib exited the men's room, Reds screamed loud enough for Gino to hear, "Looks like the rural carriers held a convention in the men's room." Gino looked at Reds and rolled his eyes. Old Man heard and saw the exchange and started singing "Love is in the air everywhere I look around."

"Yeah!"

Oliver began, "Hey, yesterday Lynn was in the restroom for a long time. Now it's Buster's turn. I guess he's gonna make an issue too about not being able to complete his route in time because he doesn't have the time."

"Yeah, right, but perhaps we shouldn't complain about him being in there. At least we are having a moment of peace while he's not out here." said Chip.

"Hey, Chip," asked Zakar, "why don't the post office make the residents that have those little five inch mail slots in their doors get bigger mail slots? I mean you can push the letter size mail through the slots, but the larger stuff like magazines and all too big. Plus the mail tears when you try to push it through."

"Well, Zakar, responded Chip, from my understanding if an existing house was originally built with those small mail slots the post office can't make them change."

"Right," replied Reds. "It's only when a new house or building is erected can the post office determine the type of delivery mode to be used…whether it's a larger mail slot in the door, or curbside delivery, or even one of those multi-unit cluster box systems."

"Very good Reds, I see all that college engineering education paid off!" said Willie.

"Yeah, good one!"

0815: Buster exited out of the men's room. "Ahhh Shoo-ee!"
"Uh oh, here we go again, get ready people, here comes another one of Buster's restroom stories." warned Old Man.

"Jimma nee ziz…uh… Shoo-ee! Man, the one thing I really hate is when you're really trying to take a dump and people are talking loud! You know what I mean? I couldn't even hear myself pass gas…I could feel it but I couldn't hear it!"

"Oh, Buster please, please, I can't bare another restroom story, they're so nasty." said Oliver.

"Yeah, yeah yeah, whatever you say little sweet Oliver. Anyway ,as I was about to say before I was so rudely interrupted, when I go to the bathroom and I'm really feeling like I'm gonna explode, and other people are in there talking, that bothers me. I don't know about you all but I like to hear myself go. I mean, how can I know how much I'm dumpin' if I can't hear myself going and dropping some?" babbled Buster.

"Yeah, good one." said Marlon.

"Oh, my God that Buster is so disgusting!" clamored Oliver.

"Yeah, I know what you mean Buster, like when you have to push real hard and you're gruntin' and all that." said Zakar.

"Yeah, sho' ya right new school…you know what I'm talking about?" said Buster. Feels like a brick…a really dry brick."

"Oh, for goodness sake he is just too disgusting for me. Now I think my stomach is gonna be sick." said Oliver.

Buster started laughing.

"Yeah, good one!"

Buster continued laughing, and then began asking, "So what happened yesterday afternoon with Lynn in the parking lot, Chippie?"

"Yeah, let's ask Chippie! He won't lie, he always tells the truth." said Marlon.

"Yeah."

"Now you guys know you ain't gonna get nuttin out of good ole Chippie. You know Chippie's not a gossiper like some of you people." shouted out Old Man.

"Yeah, unlike the rest of us, Chip's a good guy."

Chip and I looked at each other, shook our heads and just smiled.

"Man, I miss Lynn." Buster laments.

"You miss Lynn, Buster? I didn't think you missed or cared for anyone!"

"Well, actually it's not that I miss her, I just miss looking at her body! I really could use looking at a woman right about now. You married guys know how it is when your wife is out of town and you ain't seen a female body in a couple of days."

"Buster, you sure are a trip and a half!" proclaimed Rico. "I mean is there anything good in you?"

"Aw who cares what you think holy man?" responded Buster. "I've seen you looking and lusting at women. I know you Spanish cats like looking at the ladies. Especially like the ones on your route lying around at the pool in their little, skimpy bikinis, showing the world everything."

"Yeah, Rico! Tell us you don't do that. You might be married but I know you ain't dead!" shouted Willie.

"Yeah, you ain't dead Rico!"

As Rico quietly laughed to himself, Buster said, "Yeah, you go ahead and laugh holy man, you know I'm right."

"Yeah, right, whatever you say, Buster, whatever you say." replied Rico.

I walk over to Zakar and whisper to him "Zakar, please come with me to the supervisor's office."

"Oh, boy, I knew it was a matter of time. You're late Mr. V, I thought you would have taken me into the office sooner. You're untimely," said Zakar.

I could only stare at him.

"I'm sorry Mr. V, I thought I would add a bit of humor. You know gotta laugh a bit."

Chip V snickered and said, “Some people never learn.”

“Hey, Mr. V, do I need to get my union rep?” asked Zakar.

I turn to him and nod yes.

“Zakar, when it comes to you, you will always need a union rep. That’s a foregone conclusion.” responded Reds.

“Yeah, good one!”

“Funny funny Reds,” responded Zakar as he walked over to Willie, letting him know that I was taking him into the office.

Willie then yelled over to me, “What did he do now Mr. V?”

“What hasn’t he done? He oughtta be glad he has a job.” stated Old Man.

“Yeah!”

“Guys, I can’t discuss this on the floor, please come with me into the office.” I replied.

“Don’t worry Mr. V, I’ll watch the employees for you.” said Old Man.

As we walk to the office I instruct Willie to swipe his time card to union time, and Zakar to swipe his time card to other time.

We enter the supervisor's office, I shut the door behind us, "Zakar this is PDI, which may involve disciplinary action being taken against you. It's regarding your failure to report to work as scheduled. Please tell me why you once again, for the second time this week, failed to report to work as scheduled."

"Well, what time am I supposed to be here Mr. V…don't we have a five-minute leeway?"

"Zakar, you know the start time is seven thirty. We just had a discussion regarding this on Monday. Furthermore, I'll remind you that you have a settled seven-day paper suspension on file for the same issue."

"I know Mr. V, I don't know what to do! Can I help it if my girlfriend forgets to set the alarm for me? Besides, am I the only one who shows up for work late? I'm not the only one you know!"

"Well, Zakar, what time should your girlfriend have set the clock for you?"

"Usually the clock is set for six fortyfive."

"Six fortyfive?"

"Yes, six fortyfive!"

"Why six fortyfiveZakar?"

"So I can be to work at seven thirty!"

"What a minute Zakar, just a minute ago you asked me what time you're supposed to report for work? Now you tell me seven thirty. So then you know that the start time is seven thirty."

"Yeah, yeah, I know."

"So, you are saying you failed to report for work as scheduled because of your girlfriend failed to set the clock…is that your reason?"

"Yes."

"So it's your girlfriend's fault?"

"Come on Mr. V! Look, I'm sorry I was late. I know I gotta get better at reporting to work on time."

"Okay Mr. V, is there anything else?" asked Willie.

"No, that's all for right now. Gentleman, you may return back to your cases but first please make sure you swipe back to office operation on the time clock, thank you."

“Okay Mr. V, but may I first have just a minute with Zakar in private?” asked Willie.

“Yes, you may,” head out of the office and back onto the workroom floor.

“Listen here Zakar,” said Willie, “when are you gonna stop blaming everyone else for your problems? Sooner or later you’re gonna have to take responsibility for your own actions!”

“Yeah, yeah yeah, I hear ya,” replied Zakar… “but just remember your job is to fight for me not make me feel guilty.”

As I inch to my desk and I hear Oliver,”Wow Mr. V, I think you just set a new record for the shortest PDI in Creeks Bend Post Office history.”

“You should know Oliver as many times as you have been in the office.” responded Marlon.

“Hey, Mr. V, maybe you should change Zakar’s start time to eight o’clock, maybe then he would be on time.”

“Yeah, right…knowing him he’d be late at that time too!” said Rico.

“Yeah, good one!”

"Now that's not Christ-like Rico!" replied Buster. "Now you're judging the man."

"Yeah!"

0830: I give the daily safety talk. "City carriers and rural carriers please listen up! Today I want to give a safety on Avoiding Backing Wherever Possible. As you know the, our district has experienced three backing in the past ninety days. All of which were entirely preventable. Everyone in this office knows the NO-backing policy and you know that it must be strictly adhered to. However, for those times when backing is a must, and absolutely can not be avoided, you must follow these procedures. First, you must properly dismount your vehicle. Who can tell me what that means?"

Chip raises his hand…"Ooo ooo ooo, Mr. V I know…I know Mr. V!"

"What is this, the "Welcome Back Kotter," or something? Ooo ooo ooo, I know Mr. V…ooo ooo ooo," echoed Reds?

"Yeah!"

"Ok Chip, go ahead and please explain for us the proper technique to be used when dismounting the vehicle."

"Well, first you must curb your wheels towards the curb to help prevent any possibility of the truck rolling away. Secondly, you engage the parking brake. Next, you must place the gear shift into park. And finally, you have to turn off the engine and remove the key from the ignition."

"Perfect, thanks, Chip! Everyone, please give Chip a round of applause."

The clapping of the hands and whistling could be heard in response.

I continue, "Once you have secured and properly dismounted the vehicle you must then walk all the way around the vehicle to make sure there are no children and or pedestrians, or any obstacles around the truck. Once you followed these procedures and decided that it is safe to back up then you may re-enter the mail truck and proceed with caution. Please everyone; these necessary procedures have been put in place to ensure that you and anyone else who may be around you have a safe day. Now in light of what I just said always remember that it is better to back into a parking slot as opposed to pulling into one. Reason being is that when you back into a slot most times there is no traffic behind you. It is a more controlled environment. However, if you pull into a slot then you must back out of it into possible oncoming traffic. And that traffic can come from either direction. It lends to and uncontrolled situation."

"Now who can tell us our famous backing slogan?"

Willie raised his hand.

"Yes, Willie," go ahead.

"I think it's "When in doubt don't pull out!"

"Oh, you're so nasty," said Old Man!

"Yeah, good one," added Zakar!

"Yeah," said Marlon!

Everyone started laughing.

"Oh, all ya'll shut up. Ain't nothing but a bunch of sinners up in this place, including you Rico? You ain't nothing but a perpetratin' Christian. What, you think you're some holy man or something. Perhaps you should get yourself a Spanish bible instead of that English one you carry around. Maybe then you'd understand more of what you're reading…you might even become a better perpetrator…I'm out!"

"That's ok Buster I forgive you, brother. I'm not gonna stop prayin' for you. I know God can still do a good work in your heart. You're not that far gone," quipped Rico.

"Boy I don't want you prayin' for me. I want someone who really knows how to get a prayer up into heaven. A person like my father, now he was a real prayer warrior. Yup, ole Reverend Jackson…now pop could really get the church to shoutin! Boy, we used to have church. Man pop would start to feel it. You know how they do it." (And then Buster went into his Reverend Jackson impersonation.)

"Good one," said Zakar.

"Yeah!"

"Good one, good one! Is that all you know how say is good one," added Buster?

"Yeah!"

"Alright folks calm down. But seriously, the proper expression is "when in doubt don't back out."

"Well, that doesn't sound any better Mr. V," added Old Man.

"Well, whatever, you know what I meant," I replied.

It was then that postmaster Meghyn came out of her office and gave a mandatory stand-up service talk regarding "Mail not being picked up by the customer." This is when a customer's mailbox becomes full due to the customer not picking up his or her mail for several days. So Meghyn begins by saying, "Recently a couple of you have asked me what is the proper procedure when a customer's mailbox gets full and what to do with the mail. So here's what you are to do when that happens. You empty the mailbox of all the mail. Leave a slip in the mailbox for the customer stating that their mailbox was full and that their mail is being held at the post office for ten days due to their box being full. Bring all the mail back to the office place it in a mail tub, mark or label the tub, and leave it at your case for ten days. If after ten days we don't hear from the customer you must then fill out the carrier generated form "Moved Left No Forward" and return all the mail back to the sender. DO NOT, I REPEAT, DO NOT simply place the mail in the "Unable to Forward" bin, OKAY? THANK YOU!

She ends by saying, "City carriers it's now eight thirty-five and so it's time for the city carrier ten-minute office break. The clock over city route one now says eight thirty-five therefore you are to be back at your cases by eight forty-five! COMPRENDE?"

"Comprende? Hey, she's talking Spanish. She must be talking to you Rico," said Reds.

"Yeah, good one!"

"Yeah!"

"I swear, youngster, you say, yeah good one, one more time and I will jam my fist so far down your throat you'll need toilet paper to wipe your, I'M OUT," said Buster, as he started laughing.

"Oh, my gosh…gee whiz, you people are so violent," stated Rico, as he began to walk to the men's room.

"You people, what do you mean by you people," asked Willie? "You know we African Americans take offense to that stuff Rico. Don't let me file a racist charge against you, Chico?"

Rico just shook his head in amazement as he opened and walked through the door to the men's room.

"So Chippie," began saying Reds once they sat down in the swing room, "What do you think you're going to do once you retire?"

"Well, you know, I've been seriously thinking of working at a funeral home."

"What…a funeral home Chippie?"

"Yes, a funeral home. Maybe Mr. V will hire me at his place. The more I think about it the more I realize that I would probably fit in well doing that kind of work."

"That work? You mean actually working on the bodies?"

"No, not that stuff! But being a doorman and greeting the people as they come in. Hey, perhaps even driving the family cars or limousines. You know, I've always thought of myself as a customer service type person. You know, and meeting and talking to people."

"Yeah, talking to people…Is that why it takes you so long to get back from your route…all that talking to your customers, huh?"

"Hahaha, that's real funny Reds. No, I just think I can see myself doing that kind of work. Besides, when my wife Chrisy passed away and we were working with Mr. V's funeral home, they made us feel so valued. Talk about service! He and his wife were so helpful and caring. They really went over the top to care for us. They made us feel as though we were the only family they saw during that whole week, even though I'm sure they had been serving other families at the same time. They were just so personable and caring. And even after days and weeks had passed by, the funeral home would call us and just follow up with us to see how we were doing. I almost got the impression that he would do the business for free if he could afford to."

"Hey, Chip," asked Reds, "did it feel funny using Mr. V's service being he is your supervisor, and that he's a Black funeral home? I mean Blacks generally go to Black funeral homes and Whites generally go to White funeral homes."

"Oh, no, no way! It just seemed like the right choice. I mean at that time I did not personally know Mr. V, but I had heard of his work and professionalism from friends of mine and they highly recommended him and so I went with his service. Besides, who cares whether he was Black or White or whatever? If the service is right and the care is there and the price is fair that's all that should matter. That's all that mattered to me."

"Well, tell me this, would you call on Mr. V, again, to handle your funeral if you something happened to you?"

"Well, I don't think I would be the one calling Mr. V. I mean if it were my funeral I'd be dead. But my daughter would know what to do. She'd call Mr. V, it doesn't matter to us."

"Yeah, I hear ya Chip. But you know there are some people whether Black or White where it would matter. White's go to White funeral homes and Black's go to Black funeral homes. It's just the way the world is."

"Yeah, I know, you're right about that. Doesn't make it right though."

"Well, Chip you'd probably fit in well in that line of work. You're a caring, sensitive and compassionate kind of guy, but I'm sorry, I could never work around dead people, no offense Chip, but they just give me the creeps," said Old Man.

"Well, Old Man, have you ever had a dead person call you a name or give you the finger or curse you out? Have you ever heard of a dead person shooting or robbing someone? Come on guys, it's the living ones you got to watch out for," responded Chip.

"Well, you have a point there, but as for me I wouldn't be caught dead around a funeral home."

"No, you're right! You wouldn't be caught dead around a funeral home…you'd be caught dead in a funeral home."

Yeah right! Hahahaha, laughed everyone.

"But seriously, and I don't believe I'm talking about this, but when I go I'm gonna be cremated! They're not gonna string me up or hang me upside down in some prep room and drain my blood out!"

"You guys are so silly," responded Chip.

"Well, hey, if that's what you wanna do when you retire from here, you go for it! Just don't start looking at me strange when you see me walking around town."

"What, what do you mean, Old Man?"

"You know what I mean Chippie…looking at me like I'm a potential funeral customer. You know, pulling out the measuring tape and sizing me up!"

"Oh, yeah right, hahaha!"

"Well, that's what dem guys do," said Marlon.

"Yeah!"

"Ha ha ha! Don't you worry Old Man, hopefully, you still have a few years left ahead of you…or at least I think you do!"

"Oh, thanks for those encouraging and comforting words," responded Old Man.

"Hey, no problem Old Man!"

"Hey, seriously," asked Reds, "do you think funeral directors look at people as potential business? I mean really! I wonder what they think when they hear that someone is in the hospital or on hospice? Do you think they pray and ask god to heal them? Or do they start rubbing their hands together and go CHA CHING!"

"Yeah, if that's the case, I'm sure the funeral director smiles ear to ear when he sees Old Man walking around! Heck, he probably smiles wide enough he could eat a banana sideways!"

"Ha ha ha, that's real cute! You guys better hope you make it to my age," responded Old Man.

"Still though, seeing and being around all that sadness Chip, I think that would depress me," said Reds.

"Yeah, you might think that, but think about it, most times you go to a funeral and the people socialize and talk about good times they shared. Most people, to me, appear to be rather happy. It's like having a family or even a class reunion at times. And again, you just get this attitude of wanting to help people, and everyone caring for one another."

"Yeah, right, for at least the moment."

"I think funerals and the whole idea of death and dying gets us in touch with the creator," said Oliver.

"Oliver, if anyone needs to get in touch with the creator, it's you," said Willie.

"Oh, boy there he goes again."

"Well, Chippie baby that line of work would probably fit you well! I'm sure whatever you do you'll be good at it. You deserve to retire! We're gonna miss ya."

"Hey, Chip, whatcha gonna do with all that money? I mean you'll have your pension from the military and a pension from the post office. Plus you'll make some money working at the funeral home!

Dag! Perhaps you'll find it in your caring and compassionate heart to loan me some money," said Willie!

They looked at each other and said simultaneously, "Loan you money? Yeah, right!"

With that said the carriers got up from their chairs and proceeded to walk back to their cases.

Prior to the end of the carrier's ten minute office break, and Willie returning back to his case area, he approached me and said…

"Hey Mr. V, I'm sure, based on that safety talk, that you or Ms. Peggy will be out on the street today performing driver observations. If you do just make sure the carrier knows you are observing them. You know it's illegal to perform a covert operation. The carrier must be made aware that you are watching them. No spying please!"

"Come on Willie," I countered, "what's the purpose of doing street observations if the carrier knows they're being watched? Of course they'll do everything correctly if they know ahead of time that they're being observed."

"Still Mr. V, you have to let them know," he insisted. And with that he returned to his duties.

0845: The ten-minute office break is over and most of the carriers have returned back to their cases from the ten-minute office break except Zakar.

“Chip said, leave it to Zakar to now go to the bathroom AFTER the ten-minute break is over! I tell ya, some of these people could not work in traditional corporate America. They’d be fired in a minute. Good for him that there’s a union.”

“Yeah, like Ole Man always says…he oughtta be glad he’s got a job” quipped Reds.

“Hey, Buster, guess what song I heard on the radio this morning on my way to work?”

“Whatcha hear Willie?”

“The Stylistics, “Trashman didn’t get the trash today, oh why because they want more pay.”

“Whew, stop it, stop it! I love that song man. Nuttin’ like the Stylistics!”

“Yeah, what’s the name of that song Buster?”

“People Make the World Go Around,” as he sings it.

“Yeah, that’s right! Man that was a good song back in the day,” said

Willie.

"Back in the day…man it's still a good song," replied Buster.

"Hey, Witness, you're a music buff. You remember that song?"

"Yeah, that was a good one. Songs back then just seemed to have more meaning…you know, very relative to the times. Hey, Buster, how 'bout this one from the Stylistics…"You're alone all the time, does it ever puzzle you, have you asked why you seem to fall in love and out again, do you ever really love, or just pretend."

"Oh, my god, now you're singing!"

"Hey, Mr. V, can sing," said Bitsy.

"Hey, you know what was another good song?"

"What? Give us another one Mr. V!"

"Stevie Wonder's "All Is Fair In Love," I responded as I sang it.

"Ah Shoo-ee…boy, you pulling them out today Witness. Better stop man, I'm starting to get nostalgic," said Buster!

"Yeah, that'll happen with songs like that, I said. But the song I really like is Too Hot by Tom Grant. It's the piano version of the song done by Kool and the Gang. Man, that cat can play a piano. Oh, my goodness it's nasty! You gotta google it."

"Yeah, and I like this song…how's it go…oh yeah…"Hello it's me, I thought about us for a long, long time." That was by Todd Rundgren."

"Oh, that's a White song," said Willie.

"A White song…what gives Willie? Does everything have to be a Black and White issue," asked Chip?

"Yeah, what gives Willie? What does it matter," asked Marlon? "A song is a song. Besides, we White people have our songs and you people have your songs…and sometimes we all cross over, but it's all good!"

"Yeah, what's up with that stuff? Are you saying us White people can't sing or produce quality music," asked Oliver? "Willie, you people are just as racial as any other group, but because you are colored you get away with it."

"Yeah! You let one of us guys say something like that and you wanna call Rev. Al Sharpton and march around town and protest."

"Yeah!"

"I chimed back in…hey guys, that song was back in nineteen seventy-two. Boy, there were some great songs back in that era."

"Were you even born yet, Marlon," asked Old Man?

"Nope, not yet," said Marlon with a grin. "But the world somehow knew I was on my way here. All the ladies were praying and hoping for my birth."

"Oh, my gosh I think I'm gonna be sick," said Oliver.

0900: "Hey, V, is the Peacock still outside, have you seen it lately?"

"No I have not seen it and neither has anyone else since early this morning."

"Ok, well grab Mason and tell him to go outside and see if he can find it. Actually, you know what, with his lack of hearing that may not be a good idea. Suppose it sneaks up behind him. I'll call the local SPCA and see if they can send someone over here."

0915: The retail window had been open for approximately fifteen minutes and there were four people in line and one standing at the other retail window being waited on by Katie. A customer, a Japanese man, approached the window where Spice was working and informed her that he had come to retrieve a package that was attempted delivery yesterday but he was not home at the time to receive it. So Spice proceeded to ask him…

“Sir, do you have the notification slip with you?”

“YES I DO,” he said loudly in his accented English and with a big smile,”YES, I DO!”

Spice, looking at him strangely, carries on, “Ok good. Do you also have ID with you?”

“YES, Yes, I DO,” he yells, and gave Spice both the notification slip and his ID.

“Ok, sir I will be right back,” Spice responded.

“Yes, I hope you will,” replied the man.

Katie, the other window clerk as well as the customer she is waiting on, looked over at Spice as if to say, what’s up with this guy? Spice just raised her eyebrows and subtlety shook her head as she walked away to search for the package.

About thirty seconds later Spice returned to the window with the small package in her hand, and so hands the gentleman his item. Well, as she preceded to hand him the package the man quickly grabs the box, shakes it and then asks Spice and Katie …

"Do you ladies know what this is? I have been waiting four to six weeks for this to come in and it's FINALLY HERE."

Spice, hesitantly says..."No, no I don't know."

"O-o-o-h I'm so excited! Please, oh please, can you please open it for me? I'm just too excited, my hands are shaking!"

"Sir I wish I could help you but we have other customers in line and I..."

"Oh, y-e-s I understand...w-e-l-l it's my booster kit!"

"Your booster kit," asked Spice?

"Yes, my booster kit! My booster kit has finally arrived! My young lady friend is going to be happy now! My TESTOSTERONE booster kit has finally come!"

"O-o-o-kay...well that's good sir," replied Spice..."I'm very happy for you and your young lady friend."

"Oh, no, you don't understand. You see honey I'm sixty-nine years old and my lady girl she's...well let's just say she is a bit younger than I. As you probably k-n-o-w when we men get to be a certain age some things just don't...how should I say...perform the way they use to. Young lady, you have made my day! Thank you sooo much!"

The gentleman went on to say, "by the way Miss you are a very pretty young lady, tell me uh are you already taken…you know… married?

"Well, sir I'm not married but yes I'm already taken thank you," replied Spice.

"Oh yes, of course, you pretty ones usually are." He then proceeded to walk away but then he quickly turned around and asked Spice…

"By the way…uh, what is your name may I ask?"

"My name is Spice sir."

"Oooh, Spice. Well, that's a nice name are you Asian? Oh, I'm sorry I guess I'm being a bit nosey aren't I?"

Then he turned to Katie and said, "Miss, please do me a favor and tell your boss what a wonderful employee Miss Spice is. Would you do that for me please, hmmm?"

"Yes, sir don't you worry I most definitely will let the supervisor know," replied Katie!

As the gentleman worked away Spice looked over to the woman whom Katie was waiting on and said to her, "why do I always get the weird ones? Is there a sign on my head saying ALL WEIRDO'S

IN THIS LINE?"

And with that, Spice turned her head back to the retail line and said to the next customer. "Good morning, welcome to Creeks Bend post office, how may I help you today?"

"Oh, thank you. Yes, I'm here to pick up a very important package and I'm so excited…oh I'm just kidding!"

Back to the working room floor where Old Man is having a conversion with Reds, and he asked, "Hey, Reds."

"Yeah, Old Man!"

"You're into dogs, have you ever had to put any of your dogs down?"

"You mean like have them put to sleep?"

"Yeah!"

"Of course! I've had four dogs in the past twenty-five years and all of them had to be put to sleep. Probably the most painful thing I've ever had to do. I'll never get another one again."

"Me either, I chimed in. I remember my mother having to put my dog, Brutus, down. Man, I cried liked a baby! Brutus loved sleeping and taking rides in the car. Well, on his last day my mother took him to the veterinarian to be put to sleep, and all I could think of was Brutus being so happy to get into the car not knowing it was to be his last ride. I just kept thinking of him running to the car, wagging his tail…brakes my heart even now. Geez, since then I've had to put down two more dogs…just hate it! I don't think I'll ever get another dog either."

"Yeah, I know what you mean," replied Old Man. "I'm thinking of having to put my Rottie down. He's got cancer throughout his body. The vet says there's no hope, just a matter of months or less."

"Man, pets can really get close to you," responded Reds.

"Yeah, and when they look up at you with those big sad eyes, ohhh! Just pierces me through the gut knowing I'm gonna have to have him put to sleep," continued Old Man.

"Yup dogs…man's best friend," responded Reds.

"Man's best friend? What 'chu mean man's best friend," responded Willie? "How can you call a dog man's best friend? You take them for a walk, they take a dump on the sidewalk and then you gotta pick up their crap with your hands! What kinda best friend is that?"

"Yeah, what kinda friend is that," shouted Marlon?

"I tell you what," continued Willie, how about letting me be your best friend and you take me for a walk and I'll take a dump and then you pick up my crap…what cha say about that Old Man?"

Everyone started laughing.

"Oh, Willie, you just have to be a dog lover I guess," said Chip, "that's just how they are."

"You got that right Chippie, that's just how THEY are," blurted Buster! You ain't never gonna see a brother doing something like that. Hell, I ain't never had a friend ask me to pick up after him after he took a crap!"

"Yeah!"

"Boy you people are something else," responded Old Man.

Oooo, there he goes with that you people mess.

0920: Telephone rings. "Good morning, Creeks Bend Post Office Mr. V speaking may I help you?"

"Well, uh yes, I was hoping you could. Umm, I was just wondering if I brought my letter into your office would it get wet. I mean if I brought it inside to your office and mailed it from inside. It's raining out and I was just wondering if my letter would get wet."

"No sir your letter will not get wet," I replied.

"Ok good. So you are sure it won't get wet?" he continued to ask.

"Yes, sir I'm sure your letter won't get wet."

"How about where it's going, will it get wet there?"

"Well, sir I don't know where you're sending it to or what type of delivery receptacle the recipient has that you're sending it to. But it should be fine."

"Oh, yes I see. Well, it's going to the IRS."

"Well, sir I'm sure your letter won't get wet."

"Okay, so if I place it into one of your collection boxes inside the lobby my letter won't get wet right?"

"Yes, sir that's correct. This building is enclosed. This building has a secure roof and four walls."

"Oh, yes I'm sure it does," he responded. "I just didn't know if when taking it from my car into the post office if it would get wet. This letter is very important."

"Well, sir," I asked, "do you have an umbrella? Perhaps if you used an umbrella when you get out of your car it would help to protect you and your letter from the rain."

"Oh, I'm not wearied about me getting wet, just my letter. How about if I put it in a little bag, like a plastic sandwich bag, he asked?"

"Well, sir if that will make you feel better you go ahead and put the letter in a plastic sandwich bag."

"Oh, okay, great! So you think it will be okay then?"

"Sir, trust me, your letter will not get wet it will be okay."

He continued on asking…"Do you think if I put some scotch tape over the address part that would help? Someone actually told me not to do that because it might mess up the mail machine."

"No, I replied, you don't have to put tape over it. Just put it in the bag. Your letter will be fine."

"Oh, okay I see. So you're sure it won't get wet, even when it leaves your building and gets put into the truck?"

At this point, I begin to mumble under my breath…what kind of idiot is this? Then I said, "uh sir, your letter will be okay."

"I'm sorry for being a pain. I just want to make sure my letter will be okay. So you're sure it will be fine," he continued?

"Yes, your letter will be fine!"

"Well, I didn't know if there was a distance between the roof and the truck where you load the mail."

"Sir, the truck pulls up to the loading dock and the roof reaches out over the truck. Your letter will not get wet. The ceiling extends over the truck."

"Oh, good, yes I see. So you don't think it's a good idea to put tape over the address either," he continued to ask?

"No, you don't have to put tape over the address. In fact, putting tape over the address may slow down the letter processor," I informed him.

"Oh, okay really? Well, I don't want to slow down the timeliness of my letter getting to the IRS now do I? And tell me, where is this letter processor located? I assume it's indoors?"

"Sir please your letter won't get wet! Your letter will be okay! Your letter will be fine!"

"I know I'm being a pain…but…"

"Sir please, your letter will be fine."

"Oh, okay, well if you think so. You do think so don't you?"

"Yes! Yes, I think so!"

"Well, okay. Uh, what was your name again?"

My name is Mr. V.

"Oh, okay. V? How do you spell V? That's an unusual name. Is it spelled V-E-E?"

Oh, my goodness! I say to myself under my breath. Please, will this man ever give up!

"Sir, I have work I must attend to. Will that be all?"

"W-e-l-l yes I guess that's it," he responded.

I quickly said, "Okay then goodbye." And I quickly hung up the phone.

Of course, looking over at me and seeing my frustration was Reds.

So he said, "Don't worry Mr. V you'll get that big raise soon. Hey, it's all about service. Remember Mr. V, you gotta satisfy the customer. You'll get your reward in the end." He said in a sarcastic voice with a smile.

Ring ring ring. The phone rings again. "Good morning, Creeks Bend Post Office, Mr. V speaking may I help you?"

"Oh, yes, hi again Mr. V."

Oh, my goodness it was the same person calling back.

"Yes, may I help you?"

"Uh yes, uhh what time does your last collection truck leave today?"

"Five thirty PM," I replied.

"Oh, good. Well, perhaps it won't be raining by then. What do you think?"

"Sir, I don't know."

"Oh, yes right, he responded, that's several hours from now. Well, okay goodbye and have a good day!"

"–Goodbye sir!". *Oh my goodness! WHAT AN IDIOT! Uhhh! I then thought to myself, If I did find his letter I would take it and pee all over on it and then call him back and tell him..."I'm so very sorry sir but I found your letter and it got wet!"* Hey, that's just how I felt!

I hear Bitsy asking Pudgy how long she thought it would take management to post Chip's route once he's officially retired.

"I don't know Bitsy. It'll probably be a month or so. I guess it depends on how hard the union pushes the matter."

"Yeah, right, then Monique will be next in line to make regular."

"Right, unless they put a freeze on making regulars."

"Well, they could also let the other regular carriers bid on it just in case some wanted to change routes and get off the one they're already on."

"Well, knowing management they'll probably push the matter to leave his route vacant and not make Monique a regular."

"Yeah, they'll probably try that too."

"Knowing management, they may even try abolishing Chip's route and absorbing it into the other routes."

"You're probably right Pudgy. Although I hardly think the carrier union will let that happen."

0930: Carriers start pulling their routes done.

"I can't wait til next munt," said Marlon.

"Next munt? How you spell that altar boy," asked Buster?

"Yeah, spell it," said Old Man.

"M u n t…munt," quickly said Zakar as he laughed. He meant to say, next month.

"Boy! It's a good thing they didn't have a grammar section on da postal exam, else you never woulda been hired," shouted Buster.

"Hey, Willie look who's talking, Mister ruin the King's English himself," said Reds.

"Yeah, I know," responded Willie, he makes us all look bad. He's a bad representation for us Black folks."

"Yeah!"

"You guys ought to be thankful for affirmative action," said Oliver as he chuckled and said…"Oh, I was just kidding."

"Aw look now, the gay community speaks out. Boy, you oughtta be glad I don't come over there and put my foot up your you know what," shouted Buster!

"Yeah, with his sexual preferences he'd probably like your foot up there," said Marlon.

"Hey, come guys watch your mouth," said Chip!

"Yeah, good one!"

"Alright people that's enough," I replied!

"Yeah, watch your mouth Marlon, you know that's not nice," said Zakar.

"Hey, new school," shouted Reds, "what piece of the route did you get?"

"I got the good section. The one with the salon called Beautiful and Brash. Oh, my god! Have you ever been in that place Reds," asked Zakar? "The women in there are incredible! And oh my god their bodies! I think I might just get married to one!"

"Heck, whatcha gonna do then, new school, turn her into a Muslim," shouted Buster?

"Yeah, al Salama lick em," shouted Marlon!

"Hey, watch your mouth, leave my religion out of this," responded Zakar!

"Religion! What religion are you boy," asked Old Man? "I've never seen you pray. I've seen Rico pray, but I have never ever seen you pray."

"Yeah!"

"Don't you worry about what religion I am, and don't call me boy!"

"Yeah!"

"I'm a man. I pay my own rent and I have my own woman," continued Zakar.

"Oh, look, sounds like Zakar is getting a little sensitive," said Oliver, as he started to laugh.

"Oliver, are you sure you want to go there? If I were you I'd stay out of this conversation before these guys turn on you and you get your feelings hurt," said Chip.

"Yeah, Oliver, you better listen to good ole Chippie," said Old Man.

"There goes Chippie once again taking up for the socially oppressed and misfits."

1000: In walks Sam, he's a carrier supervisor from New York that's looking to transfer to this area. Apparently, he heard about Ms. Peggy going out on maternity leave and so he stopped by to eye our office. You could hear the comments as he walked through the rear double doors where the carriers were loading their trucks. Even though he had a postal employee badge on, nobody stopped him to ask who he was. It's a postal safety policy that whenever a stranger walks through the doors that someone should approach the person and ask who they are. However, most employees won't because they feel that that's management's job and not theirs, and even though safety is everyone's responsibility.

Now here's a brief description of Sam; he had the personality and stature of Louie from the hit TV show "Taxi." And actually, there was a real life postal supervisor who worked at one of post offices where I had been previously employed who truly fit that description. He literally had the same physical appearance of the TV personality Louie. Most employees, unfortunately, did not take him seriously, because of his very short height, barely five feet tall and as such he caught a lot of flack and was the target of many jokes. Upper management did not treat him well. They, in my opinion, dogged him. They gave Sam the dirty work. Some of it was his fault due to his attitude and the way he talked to people, but Sammy, as we called him, could not help his appearance or speech. He was an interim supervisor from New York who had been relocated and was looking for a permanent position at one of the nearby offices where his oldest

daughter lived. Eventually, Sammy died of a massive stroke one night after work, at home. Sammy was a time bomb waiting to explode.

"Hey, look, it's the little guy from It's A Small World," shouted Reds, as he pushed his mail cart out through the doors.

I walk up to the gentleman and introduce myself, as all employees, especially management, are encouraged to do when a visitor walks into the building. The actual procedure is to greet the individual, ask to see their employee name badge, and inquire as to the reason for their visit. It's for security purposes.

"Hi, my name is Mr. V, can I help you?"
"Yeah, I'm Sammy. I'm looking to transfer here. I hear your office has a temporary vacancy becoming available soon. Can you tell me where the postmaster is?"

"Sure. Do you have an employee badge?"

"Yes, it's right here."

"Ok great, follow me, I will take you to her."

I noticed he had a speech impediment. He talked as though his tongue was stuck to the roof of his mouth, like a cleft palate. *Oh boy, not only is he short in height, five foot one inch tall, but he has a speech challenge as well. Not a combination any supervisor in the post office wants to have. These employees are gonna eat him up!* Anyway, I take him to the postmaster's office and introduce to him to Meghyn.

"Excuse me Meghyn, this gentleman is here to take a look at our office. He's interested in Ms. Peggy's temporary vacant position."

Meghyn, sitting down at her desk with a cup of tea in her hand, nearly dropped it as she looked and saw Sammy. She paused, looked at me, then looked at him, and looked at me again and mumbled under her breath, "Are you serious…this is not going to work."

"Excuse me…what did you say?" asked Sammy.

"Oh…hi Sammy, I'm Meghyn, I'm the postmaster." she said as she stood up to offer him her hand.

Envision this, Meghyn is every bit of six foot tall with her heels on and Sammy is at best five-two. He wears his pants practically below his hip line. He has no butt. His pants appear to be too long and very baggy. Of course, this would not go well with Meghyn as she is a stickler for appearance.

Sammy came forward and stretched out his hand with those little stubby fingers to shake hers. "Hi Meghyn, I'm Sammy. I'm from New York looking to transfer into your office. I've been in the post office for thirty years of which I spent the last twelve years supervising both the clerk and city carrier crafts. I heard you were going to have a possible vacancy and so I'm very much interested in it."

That's when I looked at Meghyn and said, "Well, Meghyn I'm going back out on the floor. I will leave you two alone to chat and to get acquainted."

"Awe thanks, V, how sweet of you. I really appreciate that," she said sarcastically.

Reds approached me as soon as he saw that I was back on the workroom floor and asked, "Who is the little guy? Is he going to be Ms. Peggy's replacement?"

"I don't know Reds. Meghyn hasn't made a decision yet. This is the first time the both of them have met. And besides, I'm not sure Ms. Peggy is actually going leave."

"Oh, come on Mr. V! You know darn well Ms. Peggy is will be out for at least a year. Hell every time something happens in her family, or with her, she goes out on sick leave for months. Heck, if one of us carriers or clerks did that, Meghyn would be spitting fire down our necks!"

"Honestly Reds, I don't know what's going to happen or if this guy is going to be her replacement," I replied as I sat down in my supervisor's chair.

"Yeah, right, just like usual…management not sharing information with us. Oh, God what an environment to work in," said Reds as he walked away!

I see Katie walk over to Oliver at his case and began talking to him. When postmaster Meghyn walked out onto workroom floor and noticed Katie standing at Oliver's case and shouted, "Hey, Katie, don't hold him up, Oliver needs to pull his route down and get out of here." She continued saying to Katie, "Is the window slow? How about throwing some mail in the P.O. Box section?"

Geez, Meghyn wasn't in there long with Sam. She used the moment to gather herself and called her boyfriend Mario. Knowing Meghyn she probably needed a sanity break.

Katie chirped, "Oh, I'm sorry I was just on my way to the ladies room."

Meghyn peered over at me and shook her head in disgust, "Is it any wonder the P.O. Box section doesn't get up in time. V, these people need to know that they are getting paid to work not to talk! This is not a social club…you need to say something to her when she returns from the ladies room."

As Katie returned from the ladies room she apologized to me as she strolled by saying, "I know Mr. V, I know what you're gonna say to me. I'm sorry I hope I didn't get you in trouble. She continued, "Man you can't talk to anybody around here without getting yelled at," and she proceeded to the retail window area whistling the theme song from the Three Stooges.

1130: The last of the carriers have now pulled down their routes and have headed for the street. All of my reports AM Reports have been completed and so I got up and walked over to the Retail area to observe the clerks at the window.

While standing behind the clerks at the retail window, Katie turned to me and asked, "What now? Am I in trouble?"

I shook my head and said no and informed her I had to Window Observations. She responded by asking, "Didn't you just do some observations on us last week?"

"Yes, I did, but since we failed our last Mystery Shopper Experience I or Ms. Peggy will have to perform retail clerk observations on you folks every day for a week."

"You gotta be kidding me! Well, Mr. V, I want you to know that I get nervous when there's someone standing behind me and observing me."

"I know Katie, I'm sure you do. But I gotta do my job."

I began writing and documenting Katie's performance as she waited on the next retail customer.

"Good morning, welcome to the Creeks Bend Post Office, how I may help you today," Katie asked with a smile as she greeted the customer.

"Thank you. I need to mail this to my son in Chicago, Illinois, and I need it there by tomorrow afternoon by three o'clock. What services do you have that I can use?" asked the customer.

"Sure no problem, let's see, Chicago, Illinois! Well, you can send it via our Over Night services and it will be attempted by twelve o clock noon tomorrow."

"Oh, no," said the customer, "I don't need it attempted, it needs to be delivered! How can I have it delivered?"

"Well, you can still send it via the Over Night service and you can also request that the item be delivered without obtaining a signature at the time of delivery. The carrier will just waive the obtaining of the signature. That way the mailman will scan it delivered, and leave the package whether someone is there or not. Either way, your package will be delivered by twelve noon tomorrow."

"Great! Will I be able to track it and know it was delivered?"

"Yes, sir! Our "Overnight" service comes with a tracking number. Just go online, or even use your smartphone, type in our postal web address, click on Track & Confirm and enter the label number. It will show you the activity on your package!"

Upon payment of the transaction, Katie asked the customer if there was anything else he needed such as stamps, passport or a post office box. The gentleman said no and with that, Katie handed him a receipt and ended the transaction with warm goodbye and smile.

"May I help the next customer, please? Good morning, welcome to the Creeks Bend Post Office, how can I help you today?"

"Yes, I'd like a roll of stamps."

"Ok, would you like to super-size that order? Hahaha! Just kidding! Just a little sense of humor! I'm sorry."

"Oh, no problem, besides, with the morning I've been having I could use a little sense of humor about right now," said the lady.

"Well, good. Well, would you like a roll of the Forever Stamps?"

"Forever stamps…what do you mean by forever stamps…do they last forever or something?"

"Well, yes, in a way! They work like this. Once you buy the stamps, at the price rate they are now, they will be usable at that rate for as long as you have them, even if the price rate of stamps were to increase next week. It's kinda like locking in the price!"

"Oh, okay I see. Sure, why not, since you put it like that, I'll take a roll of the Forever Stamps. In fact, give me three rolls and here's my credit card. Hmmm, Forever Stamps that's pretty clever of the post office."

"Yeah, once in awhile the post office gets it right. Oops I guess I shouldn't have said that. My boss is standing behind me and he's evaluating my performance. Oops there I go again. I guess I shouldn't have said that either. I'm sorry, I'm just a little nervous right now. I mean with my boss standing behind me and all."

"Well, I'm sure your boss will forgive you. Hey, you just increased your sales today! Perhaps he'll give you a bonus or a commission said the lady," as they both turned and looked at me with a smile.

"Well, ma'am, will there be anything else? Do you need a passport or P.O. Box?"

"No, that will be all, thank you!"

"My pleasure ma'am, here's your receipt and I hope your day ends better than it started."

"Well, boss, how am I doing? Whoop whoop whoop whoop whoop!"

"I shook my head and said you're such a porcupine."

"So do I get a passing grade, Moe?"

"Yes, you got a passing grade. I've seen enough Katie. I'm leaving and heading out to the street now to do some street observations. But first I'm going to tell Meghyn that I think we may have just failed a mystery shopper test and it's probably going to be your fault!"

"WHAT…how so?" pondered Katie.
Hahaha, "I'm just kidding! Yuk yuk yuk! By the way, I continued, did you hear the customer said Illinois's? I hate it when they say Illinois's! Even though it's spelled Illinois, it's pronounced Illinoi without the ess sound, not Illinois."

"Yes, I did," responded Katie, "and did you notice, Mr. V that I said Illinoi?

"Yes, I did!"

1145: I inform Meghyn that I'm going out on the street to perform some street observations on the carriers.

"You're da man V…go and get them," she replied!

1300: Meghyn sees Peggy talking on her cell phone and so instructs Peggy to take Sammy with her and to do some street observations as well.

"Okay Ms. Meghyn, no problem."

Meghyn then walked over to Spice and proceeded to say…" I'll be glad when she goes on maternity leave. That will be one less headache to worry about. Actually, I hope she decides not to come back."

"Yeah, I hear ya Meghyn. But beware, you don't know who you could get in her place," replied Spice.

"Who cares…a freaking chimpanzee would be better than her!" replied Meghyn. But it looks like I may have an idea who it might be…heaven forbid."

1520: Chip stops what he is doing to drive his postal vehicle to the neighborhood clubhouse to use the restroom, and call his daughter.

Ring ring, ring ring...

"Hey, dad, how's it going?"

"Hey, Carly, all is well, and just one more day to go…yippee!"

“Are you done delivering for the day?”

“Yeah, on my route, but now I have to do a section on Lynn’s route. She called out sick today.”

“Well, after what you said happened yesterday, I can see why.”

“Yeah, I suppose. It’s just that she made her problem our problem. But, I guess that’s how it goes!”

“Yeah, right, well what time do you think you’ll be done work?”

“Oh, I’d say five thirty or there about.”

“Okay, well I’ll come over and cook you some dinner. Is there anything, in particular, you might want?”

“Ah, lets see…”

“Wait, wait, I know what you want dad…baked beans and cornbread, with hot some sausage, right!”

“You took the words right out of my mouth honey…that sounds great…thanks!”

“Sure dad you got it. I’ll see ya when you get home.”

"Alright sweetheart…I love ya!"

"Love you too dad."

1550: Marlon returned back to the office upon completing his route. He apparently ran through his route because he wanted to make sure he would be on time to make his tee team for the Thursday golf league he plays in. Anyway, as he was bringing in his empty trays and tubs, along with his collection mail, he immediately and energetically began to tell this story about an incident which had occurred today at the nursing home on his mail route.

"Hey, Spice, guess what happened today at the nursing home on my route!"

"WHAT Marlon, what happened?" responded Spice.

"Well, get this. I was on my way out the door from the nursing home and the receptionist clerk asked this lady, "Where is Mr. Johnson?" And the lady said who? And the receptionist said, Mr. Johnson, you know, the man who was just over there sitting in his wheelchair." "Then the lady, I don't know who she was. I guess she was a visitor or something, said "I pushed him outside. He was in his wheelchair and he asked me to push him outside so I pushed him out." And then the receptionist said, "oh my god, outside where?" And the lady answered, "out here…he's right outside here." Then the receptionist quickly got up out of her chair and yelled, "outside where?" "He's right out here," said the lady, "he's right out here." "So I, and the receptionist and the lady hurriedly walked outside towards the patio and parking lot looking for the man. And we looked here and we looked there but didn't see him."

"Oh, no, get out," said Spice!

"Yeah, and then the lady said, "Well, he was just here a moment ago."

"No way!"

"Yeah, then the receptionist yelled OH NO!"

Spice then put her hands up to her mouth as in shock.

"And then," continued Marlon, "I looked over to the left oh about a hundred feet away I saw this man riding in this wheelchair heading down this long curving driveway."

"No, stop it!"

"Yeah, and then the receptionist began to yell and scream saying "oh my god, oh my god." And she ran back into the nursing home screaming for help. And the man in the wheelchair just kept on rolling down the driveway in his wheelchair and was picking up speed. And I couldn't believe what I was seeing. It was like I was in shock or something."

"Oh, my God," responded Spice!

"I just couldn't move or run after him...I mean it was like I froze! And then I thought to myself, wow the wheelchair is going faster. He's going too fast. He's gonna…oh know, this guy is gonna…he's gonna run into the guardrail."

By this time, Spice's eyes are as big as grapes and her mouth is agape. Another clerk walks up and listens in.

"I mean here was this little old man," continued Marlon, "with this little bald head, in a runaway wheelchair, speeding down this long curving driveway. Finally, I started walking after him and then the lady who pushed him outside asked me "are you going to go after him?" And I turned to her and said, "Lady you better get a nurse or get some help."

"Yeah, right!"

"Wait, get this! Then all a sudden, BAM, he hit the guardrail head on. And then he flew out of the wheelchair, into the air, and over the guardrail."

"No way, stop!"

"I ain't kidding! I mean it was like watching something out of the Three Stooges! And then all of a sudden these nurses, and I think a Rabbi and the manager came running out of the nursing home and down the hill. I hurried and tried to pick up the man but the nurses yelled at me and said NO…STOP! I guess they thought he might be hurt or something. But oddly enough he only ended up with some scrapes and bruises. I know it's really not funny, but I wish you could have been there and seen it!"

"Well, what happened to the lady who pushed him outside, did she get in trouble or anything," asked Spice as she was laughing?

"No! She hopped into her car and just drove away. Like she knew she was wrong. Everyone saw her," said Marlon.

"Did anyone ask you what happened or what you saw," asked another clerk?

"Yeah, I told them that this lady had said she pushed him outside. Hey, I bet if that receptionist lady sees her again she'll probably get her in trouble," responded Marlon.

"She should…I would! That old man was probably someone's great grandfather. He could have really gotten hurt," said Spice.

"Yeah, I know," responded Marlon.

From what I heard Spice, and the other clerk who overheard the story, and Marlon were hollering and in stitches!

After telling that story and emptying his mail hamper, Marlon walked over to the registry cage, commonly know as the cage, and slid his keys and scanner under the registry cage door, since Spice and the other clerk were summoned to the retail window, and lobby area to do a lobby sweep. Lobby sweeps are performed every now and then when the line at the retail window gets too long. Basically, lobby sweeps are for customers who are only picking up vacation mail, packages, or certified letters.

Just as Marlon started walking over to the time clock to clock out Peggy hollers over to him.

"Hey, Marlon, can you go back out and help out on Ms. Lynn's route? I gotta make sure these guys to back before the final dispatch truck leaves."

"How can I do that Peggy, I gotta get to the golf course? I got a golf match this afternoon. That's why I ran through my route! I had already gotten approval this morning from Mr. V!"

"Oh, come on Marlon the team needs you," responded Peggy!

"Yeah, well my golf team needs me. I'm outta here, see ya!"

1630: Spice complains to Ms. Peggy. "Hey, Ms. Peggy, when is management going to make these carriers properly break down their mail? They should be breaking this crap down while they're out on their routes that way when they return back here it's already sorted out and the dispatch clerk wouldn't have to spend so much time breaking it down here. I mean how many times do they have to be told how to do their jobs?"

"I know Ms. Spice, their like little babies who need their hands held."

"Well, I already raised my babies and I'm not interested in raising anymore," responded Spice! "Hell, this is why dispatch takes so long. And management wonders why!"

"Hey, Ms. Spice, I have an idea. I'm gonna talk to Meghyn and see if she would allow you to do a demonstration on how the carriers should properly break down their collection prior to returning to the office. Whatcha think?"

"Come on Ms. Peggy, are you serious? First of all, I ain't doing no demonstration or training no carriers on how to do their job…that's your responsibility! Secondly, Meghyn would look at you like your crazy. She already thinks you're an idiot!"

"Gee whiz Ms. Spice, you didn't have to say it like that, but I guess your right. Thanks for breaking it to me gently, I really appreciate that! Well, I would help you with that but you guys would file a grievance." said Peggy.

"Yup, that's right! And the union would get more free money from the post office. I tell you what Ms. Peggy, I have an idea…"

"Uh oh, here we go," thought Ms. Peggy."

"Why don't you do your job of supervising instead of talking on the phone to your children, maybe then the carriers would do their jobs. Huh, Ms. Peggy, how 'bout that idea?" shouted Spice.

"Oh, Ms. Spice, you don't have to be so nasty. Show a little love," said Peggy, as she turned and walked away.

"Uh huh, typical manager, not worth a dime," said Spice.

1745: The last few carriers are finally starting to come back. And as thought, they have missed the last dispatch truck by at least forty-five minutes. Guess who had to run the collection mail down to the plant? Yup, Ms. Peggy sent the new guy Sammy to the plant with the late returning mail. She had given him a map and some directions on getting to the plant. Sammy was rather reluctant to do it but he did it anyway. It would have its repercussions. Ms. Peggy went home.

CHAPTER THREE

DAY THREE, Friday

0445 - 0530: I'm performing my usual morning duties. The clerks are busy at work sorting the mail and talking about their families.

0530: The 2nd transportation truck arrives and the driver, Rodney, continues his complaining about the rear dock as it's difficult for him to unload his with the condition that the dock is in and the temporary makeshift lift. "When are these guys going to finish this dock work? These guys are lazy. Why don't they hurry up and get the job done? They spend more time down at the convenience store than you can shake a stick at. Man, you can tell they get paid per hour!" He then stops venting, closes the rear door of his truck and heads back to the plant to retrieve our third and last transportation of mail.

0535: Chip's phone sounds off. It's Carly and she's five minutes late.

"Hey, honey good morning."

"Good morning dad. I know I'm five minutes late, sorry! I had a late night…was up planning for the wedding"

"Oh, Carly, no problem, I ain't keeping tabs. Besides, it's "Thank God it's Friday! A new chapter in our life is about to begin!"

You go get 'em, dad! And don't forget in your excitement to call me when you're done your route, okay!

"You know I will sweetheart...I love you."

"I love you too dad. Goodbye…oops sorry, I meant I'll talk to you later!"

"Hahahaha right, I'll talk to you later."

0600: I receive a call from Ned Wagon, manager of the Vehicle Maintenance Facility (VMF) stating that they are bringing truck # 1845 back and will be picking up truck # 2031 to perform a routine periodic vehicle inspection.

0620: Phone rings…*ring ring ring ring.*

Okay, here we go, it's probably Lynn calling out to inform me that she's not coming in today too. I knew it, I knew she wouldn't be in today. I pick up the phone, "Gooood morning, Creeks Bend Post Office may I help you?"

"Hey, Mr. V."

Sure enough, it was Lynn. "Good morning Lynn," I said.

"Mr. V, I just wanted to let you know that I will be in today, okay?"

"Oh…you will?" I responded.

"Yes, I will."

"Okay Lynn, thanks for calling and letting me know."

"Alright Mr. V. See you when I get there." And the phone went click.

Wow...oookay! I guess this is going to be a good day. However, I will have to perform an investigation with Lynn later this morning regarding the incident in the parking lot on Wednesday, as well as the customer call when received concerning her possible indecent and unacceptable activity during her lunch break.

0630: I hear the opening of the back door next to postmaster's office. It's Meghyn arriving to work. Also, the telephone rings again. "Good morning, Creeks Bend Post Office, Mr. V speaking, may I help you?"

"Hey, Mr. V.," I immediately recognized the voice, it was Chip. "Mr. V, are you there?" I paused, as he had caught me off guard. I had quickly thought to myself…great, so Chip is calling out on his last day of work.

"Yes, Chip, I'm here, what's up?"

"I really don't feel well Mr. V. Sorry but I'm calling out sick. I know it's my last day and you probably are thinking, yeah right! But I just can't make it in. I'm so sorry!"

"Well, Chip it's not like I can write you up or something now, can I? I mean what can I say…what can I do?"

"Oh, come on Mr. V! I'm just kidding. I'll be in. I just wanted to pull your shoes and add some excitement to the start of your day."

"Oh, you dirty dog. I have to admit, you had me for a minute," I responded.

"Yeah, I bet I did. Well, I'll be in shortly. Actually, I just wanted to see how the situation was looking on my last day. I really was hoping to have a no issue day," he answered.

"Oh, Chip, it's horrible today, it's like Murphy's Law…whatever could go wrong has gone wrong. I'm gonna need big help today to get all this mail delivered! I'm sorry, but it's going to be another long day for you."

"What! You gotta be kidding me," Chip replied.

"Yes, yes Chip, I'm kidding! Now I got you!"

"Yup, Mr. V, now you got me. See ya in a bit."

"Okay Chip, we'll see you when you get here. Bye!"

I then get up to go to the men's room.

0640: Postmaster Meghyn walks out onto the workroom floor. As usual, I'm not at my desk and she throws up her hands as Bitsy and Samantha look over at her. Nevertheless, Meghyn walks around to inspect the situation.

Eventually, I walk out of the men's room and back to my desk. Out of the corner of my eye I see Meghyn walking towards me with heels clicking. She had on another tight outfit that clung to every curve of her body like second skin. It was a black dress made of some thin knit like material. It was definitely a bit too revealing to be wearing around here.

"Oh, good morning, Meghyn!"

"Good morning V!"

I then ask to her, "Meghyn, how in the world did Mario (he is her significant other) let you out of the house this morning with that outfit on?"

"Yeah, I know," she said, and then just simply flashed this big smile at me and began to say…"Yeah, yesterday on my way home I drove through a construction site with my convertible roof down. All the guys just stopped what they were doing and just stared and at me as

I drove through. Oh, I was sooo embarrassed, she said chuckling. When I got home I told Mario but he just looked at me and got mad."

She smiled again, and then she quickly changed the subject and asked me…

"Oh, by the way, did you hear about the postal motor vehicle accident yesterday afternoon?"

"No, what accident?" I replied.

She then proceeded to tell me, "Well, apparently a rural carrier from another other post office drove his postal vehicle into a low-hanging branch while attempting to deliver a package and mail to a customer's front door. Apparently, the rural carrier insisted that he never saw the branch. Well, the impact with the branch shattered the windshield and slightly crumpled the upper right corner of the roof of the vehicle."

"What," I exclaimed? Was the driver hurt?" I asked.

"No, responded Meghyn, at least not initially, but he later complained of having a stiff neck so the evening supervisor, some new supervisor, I don't know his name, took him to the emergency room to be checked out."

"I guess he got home late!"

“Yes, he did, said Meghyn, I’m sure he did.” She continued to say, “Of course, pictures were taken and the routine accident report was filled out by the supervisor. By the looks of the damage done to the truck, the driver had to have hit a huge branch. You known, the branch was hanging low and apparently he did not see it. Drove right into it!”

“Do you think he was fingering the mail as he was driving,” I asked?

“No, that doesn’t appear to be the case. According to the police officer that responded to the accident scene, it looks like he may have been talking on his cell phone at the time.”

“Why do you say that?”

“Well, the driver’s cell phone was on the floor near the foot break. It probably fell out of his hand at the point of impact. The guy must have been so shaken that he forgot to pick up his cell phone from off the floor.”

“So how did the police get there, who called them?”

“The postal customer at the house where he was attempting to deliver the mail heard the accident, called nine-one-one, and then ran out to the truck to check on him. I guess with her checking on him and trying to calm him down and all until the emergency vehicles arrived, he just simply forgot about his phone.”

"So did the officer look at carrier's cell phone?"

"Yes, it sounds like he did!"

"Oh, goodness, I bet the officer saw evidence of him talking on the phone about the time of the accident."

"Yep, I think so! Thank heavens it wasn't this office. We've been on the radar enough this year." "Well, V," continued Meghyn, "you know what you have to do…I want you to give a safety talk later this morning to all the carriers and especially the rural carriers regarding the accident. You know, she continues, are they paying attention, do they have mail in their hands or on their laps while driving? Are they talking on their cell phones…you know the deal?"

"Yes, Meghyn I will take care of it." I replied.

"Oh, and by the way, have you heard any more from Lynn? Is she coming in today?"

"Yes, as a matter of fact, she called this morning to say she would be in."

"Good, then make sure you to take her into the office as soon as she and the union representative clocks in. I want to know her side of the story. That is disgusting…boy, I'd love to fire her! How can people do stuff like that? Uhhh!"

"Well, Meghyn, let me first do the investigation and find out what happenedYou know how the saying goes, it's "innocent until proven guilty, not guilty until proven innocent." I reply.

"Yeah, right whatever," she responded with that Meghyn full of pearly whites.

0645: We had one route again to split today. This was due to Buster being out on an already approved scheduled vacation day. I scheduled one carrier to show up early so he could begin casing up the route and getting it ready to be broken up and taken to the street by the various carriers. Again, this route would be expected by management to be carried on under time or pivot time due to declining mail volume. Thank god Lynn had returned back to work or else I would have been splitting three routes instead of two. Not necessarily an easy task.

During the summertime months, May thru September, the mail volume is particularly light. This time is also known as "Prime Time Vacation" so management will allow more employees to be off per day than at any other time of the year. Since mail volumes are lower it is easier to split up the routes and have them delivered and carriers back to the office prior to the last transportation/dispatch truck leaves for the plant. Individual post office budgets are leaner at this time of the year as well.

Note: I have notice that when the mail volume is "light" the carriers pace themselves and take their time casing up the mail thus delaying the departure to the street and falsely expanding their work hours. For a few good carriers, it doesn't matter what the volume of mail is they simply do their job and say "it is what it is." However, on the other hand, when the mail volume is heavy the productivity is better.

0650: Rico walks through the doors, strolls over to his carrier case, as he always does, sits down begins to eat his cereal and reads his bible and then silently prays. I'll tell ya, you definitely need prayer around here to help maintain your sanity.

0655 - 0700: As always I pull and download the daily reports from the previous day for observation of individual carrier performances. There is also a discussion with the postmaster regarding the morning operation.

Since Meghyn had informed me yesterday that she would have cake and punch present for Chip's appreciation award and recognition speech, we made several adjustments to the clerk operation. This enabled the distribution of mail to be completed in a timely manner and available for the carriers so that they would not be delayed in leaving the office for the street.

0700: Some more carriers, the usual early ones, show up early and they are immediately instructed to clock on and help with the spreading and staging of the mail since function four, the distribution/clerk side, were running behind. A grievance will be filed by the clerk union since we recently abolished two clerk positions because upper management looked at the "numbers" and decided that we had two too many clerks. The union's hope was that through the filing of such grievances they would be able to revert the decision and thus regain the lost positions.

0715: Telephone rings. "Good morning, Creeks Bend Post Office, Mr. V speaking, may I help you?"

"This is Big Al down at the plant. Last night, a gentleman dropped off two tubs of mail to the dock but failed to bring along the required late returning collection mail slip for the dock supervisor to sign. So I need to talk with the postmaster. Is she in?"

"Yes, she is, however, I'm a supervisor, is there something that I can do for you or any questions that I can answer?"

"No, I need to speak with your postmaster per the District Manager's directive."

Uh oh, what did Peggy do now? Don't tell me she sent the new guy to the plant. So I proceeded to intercom Meghyn.

"Yeah, V, what's up?"

"It's Big Al from the plant on line one for you."

"Okay, thanks."

Five minutes later, Meghyn stomps out of her office. "CAN YOU BELIEVE WHAT THAT LITTLE HUSSY DID LAST NIGHT? She sent the new guy, Sammy, to the plant with the missed truck collection mail. What an IDIOT! What was she thinking! Uh, I'm so livid V, I don't know what to do! What's Peggy's home phone number? I'm gonna call her right now. Uh, she drives me absolutely crazy! I swear I'm going to fire her if it's the last thing I do!"

Oh, boy, here we go…Ms. Peggy strikes again!

0730: All other scheduled carrier's clock into work and begin the daily routine.

0735: Per Meghan's instructions, I take Lynn into the office and question her regarding the events on Wednesday. I took the carrier union rep, Willie, and Lynn, and ventured to the supervisor's office. "So Mr. V, what is this about, why am I being brought in here?" asked Lynn?

"Good morning Lynn, I need to conduct a PDI with you regarding the occurrences on Wednesday in the postal parking lot as well as a phone call we received from a postal customer. Please keep in mind that this investigation may or may not result in disciplinary action being taken you."

"What? You mean to tell me that you're gonna take disciplinary action against me! After I came into work today? What the hell…I could have stayed home today. But I knew you would be short handed so I came in, even though I didn't feel like it! And now you're talking about taking action against me? What an ungrateful person you are!"

"Thank you Lynn, I appreciate it." I responded sarcastically.

"Yeah, right! You certainly have a strange way of showing your appreciation! It's no wonder people go postal!"

"Whoa Lynn that sounds like a threat," I answered back.

"Hey Lynn watch that," quickly reacted Willie, "you can't say things like that. That's not good. Mr. V, please disregard her comment, you know Lynn didn't mean any harm," said Willie as he rolled his eyes.

"Listen, Lynn," I continued, "let's not make this any more difficult than it has to be. I have to conduct this investigation due to the seriousness of the situation on Wednesday in the parking lot and the phone call we received from a postal customer."

"Let's not make this any more difficult than it has to be? How is this difficult for you? I'm the one on trial here! I'm the one who was humiliated on Wednesday!"

I turn to Willie the carrier shop steward and asked him…"Willie, do you want to take a moment and calm her down?"

"Lynn, let him do what he feels he has to do…let him ask his questions." responded Willie.

"Well, go ahead Mr. V, ask your stupid questions." jibed Lynn.

"Please explain to me what happened on Wednesday, two days ago, in the postal parking lot upon your arrival back here to the office."

"What happened? Didn't Ms. Peggy tell you what happened? I told her to let you know. Can't an employee ever get some cooperation from management? My goodness, I was verbally assaulted and practically mugged by this crazy woman. Where was management when I needed protection? I could have been seriously injured!"

"Tell me who it was that assaulted and practically mugged you."

"I don't know her name. I never saw her before!"

"Why do you think she, as you say, assaulted you?"

"What do you mean by as you say? You think I'm lying to you?"

"No, I just want to know why you said she assaulted you."

"Why don't you ask her? You're the investigator!"

"Ask who? I would if I knew who she was. Do you know her name or who she was?"

"Listen Mr. V, I'm not hurt. I was a little shaken then but I'm ok now. Can't we just drop this? I'm not going to file any charges against her."

"Well, how could you file any charges if you don't know her name or even know who she is?" I asked.

She just stared at me, and then over to Willie the shop steward. I think she realized she had said the wrong thing. Nevertheless, she did not answer my question. Finally, after that brief pause, she then continued to say…"Besides, I was on my lunch break so what gives? I can do what I want to on my personal break time."

"So are you saying that the situation did happen?"

"No no, oh no, I'm not saying that. Look Mr. V do what you want to do, I'm not answering any more questions."

"Okay, well then please tell me where you took lunch on that day?"

"What day?"

"Wednesday, that same day!"

"I took lunch at my usual lunch spot."

"What is your usual spot and what time did you take lunch?"

"You know, I took lunch at my authorized location…at the time allotted according to my route book. It was about twelve-thirty. You can look in the route book at my carrier case. Heck, you're the supervisor, you should already know that information."

"Please tell me, Lynn, what is your postal truck number?"

"I don't know…it ends in something like 3777 I think."

"Well, Lynn, please explain to me why there's over an hour gap between your last stop before lunch and your first stop after lunch? It's an hour and ten minutes."

"Where do you see that Mr. V?" she asked.

"It's on your daily scanner report." I replied.

"Hey, Mr. V, you know we the union, we don't acknowledge those reports as being legitimate," said Willie. "You have no basis with those things."

"Look Mr. V, she responded, "I'm not answering any more of your questions. You go ahead and issue your discipline. It will get tossed out of my file in a couple of months anyway. Talk to my union rep."

"So that's all you have to say? You're not going to say anymore?" I asked.

"Nope, I ain't got nothing else to say. Do what you want to do. I don't care", responded Lynn.

"Look, Lynn," I replied, "This is very serious. We received a phone call from a postal patron, a witness, stating that he saw you get out of your postal truck and get into a van. He stated that you were in the van for nearly an hour. What were you doing? Why did you exceed your lunch break time without having permission to do so?"

"I don't know what you're talking about. I took my lunch break and that's what I did. That's it, nothing else...I'm not saying anything else."

Willie then said to her, "Lynn you gotta answer his questions. Don't you have anything to say in your defense? I mean if you don't give me anything how can I represent you?"

"Nope, that's it! Besides Willie, your job is not to make me say anything! You're supposed to just make sure I don't say anything wrong."

"Okay then," I replied, "If that's it and you insist on not saying anything more, then the both of you may report back to your office duties. And please make sure you swipe back into the office function on the time clock. Thank you."

"Mr. V", replied Lynn, "I have to go to the bathroom first!"

Lynn stared me down as she walked out of the office and went to the ladies room. Willie, walking out behind her, looked at me and without saying a word and rolled his eyes as if to say, can you believe this. Then he turned back around to face me and asked…

"Mr. V, do have a minute, can we talk for just a moment?"

"Yes, what's up," Willie?

"So what is Meghyn gonna do? I mean is she gonna try to remove Lynn? You know she can't do that. Besides, any discipline issued to her must be corrective in nature and not punitive. I mean just jumping to removal, the union is not gonna stand for this mess. Heck, we need to talk to the witness, and anyone else who may have seen something, if there was anything to see, replied Willie.

"I know Willie. Right now I'm just gathering information. We have to do our investigation. We'll see what happens. Besides, it won't be Meghyn issuing any discipline, it will be me. You know the deal, Willie!"

"Well, as long as you know, Mr. V, any severe discipline issued to Lynn will not stand. It'll get thrown out. You're better off giving her a discussion and leave it at that. It'll save us all time and it'll save the post office money grievance money. Besides, if I can get Lynn off of this I might have a shot at her," he gave a chuckle.

"What a representative you are Willie, I'm sure Lynn has total confidence in you. Listen, we'll wait and will see. Right now Lynn's not saying anything more and so I will gather my facts. I'll let you both know. As for now, I gotta get back out on the floor. This part of the investigation is over."

0740: I begin going around to the carriers and given them their daily instructions. I experience the usual opposition as any other day. Yes, there are a few carriers who are very obliging. One, in particular, is a female carrier known as "Tammy Jo." She's another carrier on Rural Route number four. Tammy Jo has been on vacation for the past few days so she has not been around until today. Oddly enough rather than take the whole week off she turned back a few days of her vacation time. However, knowing her I'm not surprised. Tammy Jo is a well-liked employee. Probably the most liked employee in the office, especially by the men. From what I hear, she was a "humdinger" at the other post offices where she had previously worked. She put in for two transfers before eventually arriving here. Let's just say she messed with other women's property. She has a reputation that she is not ashamed of. And I will leave it at that. That being said, she along with Bitsy, are two of the hardest working postal employees that I have ever met.

0750: "Hey, Tammy Jo," asked Zakar, "why did you come in to work today?"
"Yeah, I would never have come back to work on a Friday," responded Marlon.

"First of all, I didn't come in to work. I'm just trying to save some vacation hours so I can use it later on. Besides, today is Chip's last day and so I baked a cake for him."

"Hey, Tammy Jo tell me, just how many guys have you baked cakes for. What's the number up to now?" asked Reds"

"Well, you can rest assure she's never baked for Chippie before… he's an angel. Jezebel's and angels don't hook up."

"Hey, Tammy Jo, why didn't you wear your little black and white maid outfit!" hollered Willie.

"Hey, what you trying to say about TJ," asked Marlon?

Willie replied by singing, "If you don't know her by now, you will never never never know her ooo ooo ooo ooo"!

Chip shouted over to Willie and said, "You people are terrible."

"Hey, I told you before about that you people stuff! You know we don't play that mess," exclaimed Willie!

"Oh, Willie, give me a break. You know I didn't mean anything by that."
Tammy Jo, being used to the comments just smiled and laughed.

"See, look, there's no shame in her game," shouted Willie.

"Yeah!"

0800: Even though he was scheduled off today, Buster came in to wish Chip well. Of course, Buster, slammed the door as usual.

"Oh, no, look who it is, it's Buster! I thought we might have some peace today. What is he doing here?"

"Yeah, well I guess you thought wrong, huh youngster?"

"Yo Mr. V!"

"Sorry, I'm busy!"

"Yeah!"

"Hey, I think everybody is here today. Lynn, Tammy Jo, and Buster, all came in to say goodbye to Chippie."

"Yeah, it would have been better if Buster and Meghyn had stayed home."

"Ooooo…you better watch out Zakar. You don't want Meghyn hearing you say that."

"Yeah!"

"Hey, Marlon, were you able to get your round of golf in yesterday?"

asked Old Man.

"Yeah, I did. Boy, it started to pour right after I sank my last putt on the eighteenth hole. It was for birdie…and I made it!"

"I wonder how they came up with the progression of those golf terms?" asked Oliver. "It seems to me it should go birdie, hawk and then eagle. I mean, the term ace just doesn't seem to fit."

"Hey, Oliver, guess what, you don't fit!"

"Yeah, Oliver, you're a misfit!"

"Yeah!"

"Awe come on guys, leave Oliver alone. He's just trying to understand golf terminology."

"Oh, yeah, leave it up to Chippie on his last day to run to Oliver's defense."

"Hey, guys, it doesn't matter whether it's Chip's last day or not, he would run to anyone's defense, that's just how he is. Don't be a good person hater." responded Rico.

"Hey, I've never seen such a storm come up so fast as the one did last night. All of sudden the sky turned black and then it got real gusty. Trees were bending and branches were snapping from the force of the winds. Heck, I saw a tree get uprooted and fall over across the parking lot. It just missed hitting a car."

"Hey, Mr. V, you're a philosopher, what do you think about that."

"All I can say is that just as storms can reveal the weakness in a tree, so the storms of life can reveal our weaknesses or prove our strengths."

"Ooops, der it is. Mr. V's spiritual insight for the day, Marlon responded"

"Yeah," thank Mr. V for our "daily bread" lesson. "Hey, now Rico, he don't have to read his bible tonight, shouted Marlon, Mr. V has already given him his bible lesson for the day."

"He don't? What kind of English is that Marlon?"

"Yeah, Marlon, you should have said, **he won't** have to read his bible tonight," responded Oliver.

"Hey, Oliver how come you gay guys always talk with such proper English?"

"Hey, watch that!"

"Yeah!"

0815: "All employees may I have your attention please, I asked? "I need for everyone to gather around the parcel staging area for a brief safety and plan talk. Please hurry. Thank you."

Upon my completion of the safety talk, Postmaster Meghyn steps up to the front and begins addressing the employees by saying,

"Everyone, today it is my sad but distinct privilege to present to someone who has demonstrated professionalism and consistent, high-quality mail service to our postal delivery area and customers for over twenty-two years of postal service. Not only that, but he also honorably served his country in the military for twenty years. This individual consistently performed at a high level of productivity and accuracy despite pressure from his peers. He has reported to work for the past twenty-two years without having a single incident of unscheduled absences and has time after time performed his duties, both in the office as well as on the street, without a single industrial or motor vehicle accident. Nor were there any customer complaints of misdelivered mail ever made according to his employee file. Truly a remarkable and rare feat! Today I stand before you to present this plaque of appreciation for excellent customer service as well as this letter of appreciation from the District Manager himself. Please let's all give a round of applause to our very own, Chip!"

Speech Speech Speech!!!

Chip, obviously moved with emotion gathered himself for a moment, and finally started to speak.

"Well," he said with a gentle smile, "I guess this is what it feels like. I've seen many employees come and go and several actually retire and I always wondered what it would feel like and what I would say. Now that it's finally here…he gets a little choked up again…I don't know what to say. I'm truly at a loss for words. He pauses again... however, I will say this, I guess the thing that really kept me going, at least for the past twenty-two years was that I knew that some day, after the birth of my daughter Carly, I would need to save up money for her college years and of course, her impending wedding day. I actually kept those two events taped to my carrier case as a daily reminder. And you know…it actually worked! However…I must confess…my heart is heavy because as you all know…Chrisy…my wife who passed away three years ago of breast cancer…he paused to gather himself…is not here today to witness this moment…another pause...his eyes teary red. Nor will she see our daughter Carly get married…Chrisy and I always talked about when we would see the day come when we would give Carly away in marriage. And we often talked about seeing the day when we both would retire and we would buy an RV and spend our end years traveling across the country and driving into the sunset. Well, I guess…uh ummm…I guess…ummm…this is it."

And then there was another pause as his voice quivered.

He gathered himself again and continued, "I'm reminded of a quote I once read in the bible. I once heard my pastor say in church…it goes something like this "To everything there is a season, and a time for every purpose under the heaven." "Well, I guess my time has come!"

"I know Chrisy would be proud of Carly completing college, and happy for me that this day has finally arrived. I truly miss her. And you know what, believe it or not, I'm going to miss this place too."

"We're all going to miss you too Chip," a couple of the employees said.

Chip continued…"I know that for many of us employees there came a time in our postal career when they literally began to hate the walls in which we worked, and then eventually we became accustomed to them. Ultimately we came to accept this postal life and…the walls so much that we could not see ourselves outside of them. I must admit I came close to that mindset as well. **However…I'm sooo glad this day has finally arrived!** In closing I guess I will finish by saying as the postal adage goes, old mailmen never die they just keep on delivering! **Thanks to everyone!** And I will see you guys tonight at the Creeks Bend Tavern for my retirement **PARTY!"**

With that, Chip lifted his arms up in victory style, waving them in the air as if he had won a championship game.

Applause was given and a few tears were shed by a few. Heck, even big ole tough Buster shed a few. You know, even though Buster could easily qualify as the office jerk, there's something fun and strangely likable about him. It's as if the environment looks forward to seeing him every day. His antics seem to help the work mornings go by. This is a strange place indeed.

0830: The city carriers take their ten-minute office break. The postmaster brought a cake and punch for the office. Despite the time of celebration, the carriers are reminded that it is still a ten-minute break.

0840: Most of the carriers returned back from their ten-minute office break. However, a few extended it. You always have that small percentage who will take more than what is allowed.

0841: I take a call from a customer inquiring about a package that had been "attempted" for delivery yesterday but, according to the mail carrier, no one was home so the carrier left the pink notification card in the mailbox with the customer's other mail. However, the customer wanted to know why the carrier failed to deliver the package as the customer insisted that he was home. The conversation went something like this…

"Good morning, Creeks Bend Post Office Mr. V speaking may I help you?"

"Yes, I'm a postal customer of yours and I live at 44 Pond View Terrace. Yesterday the mailperson came by and left this pink card in my mailbox indicating that I had a certified letter that was sent to me from my late mother's Estate Attorney. However, your employee never knocked on our door nor did he ring our doorbell and I want to know why!"

"Well sir, without actually questioning the carrier, I'm afraid I would not able to tell you. But I do apologize for that. May I please have your name?"

"Yes, you may. My name is Saharadin and I have lived at this residence now for nearly a year and I must say that our mailman is, to put it lightly, not the sharpest tool in the shed!"

Of course, he was referring to, you guessed it, good ole Habib.

"Whenever we have a special delivery package or a letter needing to signed, the mailman never knocks on the door nor does he ring the doorbell! I and my partner operate a business out of our home and one of us is almost always here."

"Again, Mr. Saharadin I greatly apologize."

"Well, that's all fine and dandy but I'm a handicapped individual and it is very inconvenient for me to come to down the post office to pick up an item that could have been handled in a more professional and caring manner. You know we live on the outskirts of town in the rural area."

"Well, Mr. Saharadin may I please place you on hold while I check on the item for you?"

"Sure, and what did you say your name was," he asked?

"My name is Mr. V."

"Well, Mr. V you may place me on hold but I want to know what you are going to do about this. I refuse to be inconvenienced any more than I've already been. Getting into my van and taking a needless trip down to your post office! This by far is not the first time this has happened. I've called several times before and have made complaints…nothing changes! Heck, I believe I have spoken to you before regarding this same situation."

"Mr. Saharadin, do you have the slip in your possession?"

"Yes, I do."

"Can you please read me the article or tracking number? That way, I can look it up in our system."

"Yes, just a minute…hmmm hmmm hmmm…okay, the number is RV000321456IN."

"Okay, Mr. Saharadin I have the information right here. The item is here at the post office. Would you like for me to send it back out to you today with the mailman for redelivery?"

"Well, of course, I would. That's the least you people could do! However, I still want the matter to be addressed by you or someone up there at your office so that I and or my partner do not have to continue to go through this poor service. I almost take it personal!"

"Yes, Mr. Saharadin I understand. I promise you that I will address this matter as soon as I hang up with you. However, sir, your item will be re-sent out to you today with your regular mail delivery and I do apologize for the inconvenience and unsatisfactory service."

"That's fine. Please make sure the mailman either knocks or rings the doorbell!"

"Yes, Mr. Saharadin, I will instruct the mailman to do so. Is there anything else I can do for you today?"

"No thank you. I just want you people to please give me reasonable service…Thank you!"

I was about to say, "You're welcome Mr-" but the phone went click.

"Hey, Mr. V!" shouted Marlon.

"I'm busy!"

"Yeah right, good one! Just tell me what time that machine of yours says I should be leaving for the street?"

"Marlon, you should be leaving for the street once you have all your mail cased up and pulled down," chimed Chip.

"Hey, who made you boss?"

0850: The retail window has been open now for twenty minutes. A line of several customers waiting to purchase new passports or renew the ones they already have has formed in the lobby and there are other customers already being served at the two retail windows.

0900: "Good morning Creeks Bend!"

It's Ms. Peggy, she reported to work one hour early today, probably to impress Meghyn. She walked over to Chip to give him a hug.

"Oh, Chip, we are surely going to miss you. Come on, you can't leave us! Are you sure you wanna do this?"

"Yes, Ms. Peggy, my time has come…I gotta move on. Are you going to be here when I get back off my route?"

"Yeah, I'll be here. Unlike you Chip, I have to stay here. But yes, I'll be here when you get back."

"Okay, I'll see you then," Ms. Peggy.

"Alright, Chippie I'll see you later." as she tickled him around his waist.

Meghyn walked out of the ladies room. I can hear the heels clicking.

She smiles as she walks by. Marlon returned with his own smile, following her with his eyes. She made her way to her office Meghyn took a quick glance at the monitor in her office videotaping the lobby and sees the line of passport customers. "V intercom ten!" I pick up the phone and dial intercom ten.

"Yes?"

"Have you seen Kwan, there's a line of customers waiting in the lobby? She should have been here by now. Call her house and find out where she is! This is ridiculous! I want you to do a pre-disciplinary investigation done on her! I know Peggy just walked in but I don't want her to do it, she'll find a way to screw it up."

Kwan, the retail/secretarial clerk has once again failed to report to work as scheduled and it's now nine fifteen and she is thirty minutes late. I attempted calling her cell phone and when that failed I called her house line. In either case, I was unable to reach her and so I left a voicemail message asking her to please give us a call as to her whereabouts and when she might be arriving to work.

As soon as I hung up from trying to reach Kwan by phone I observed her quietly clocking in at the time clock, in her normal meek fashion. Then she proceeded to walk along the perimeter of the interior wall to the office where she performs many of her clerk secretarial duties. She puts her purse and lunch to set up her passport table to serve the customers waiting in line. It was as if she didn't want to be noticed. I go to inquire as to why she was late reporting to work today and failing to call informing us that she would be late. As things typically go around here, she gives a half baked excuse by saying…

"I'm sorry Mr. V but my husband, who gets up before me, forgot to reset the alarm for me."

That's not the first time I've heard that excuse, I said to myself. I then tell her go over to the time clock and swipe onto the clerk other function and to meet me in the supervisor's office.

Though Kwan is very apologetic, I go and get the clerk union steward Bitsy and instructed her to move to clerk steward time so that I could perform a PDI on Kwan. This has been the third time this month that she has reported late for duty.

PDI scene with Kwan: She walked into the supervisor office with her head down, back slightly slumped and hands folded in front of her chest.

"Good morning Kwan."

"Yes, Mr. V."

"Kwan, this is a pre-disciplinary investigation regarding the three counts of tardiness you have experienced this month. This investigation may or may not result in disciplinary action being taken against you."

"Excuse me Mr. V, but what do you mean by tardiness…what is this word tardiness?"

"He means you were late Kwan. Tardiness is another word for being late for work," Bitsy replied.

"Oh, oh ok, I'm sorry Mr. V…I just didn't know what you meant by that."

"Can you explain to me Kwan why you have been reporting late to work?"

"No Mr. V, I can't. I'm just tired. My husband forgot to reset the alarm and my house is a mess. And I my health," she starts to choke up, "is not the best it could be. I have some female problems."

"That's okay Kwan, you don't have to share it all." said Bitsy.

"Well, Kwan, do you know what your start time is?" I asked.

"Yes, Mr. V, I know it."

"And is the weekly clerk schedule, including your start time, clearly posted next to the employee time clock."

"Yes, Mr. V, it is."

"So you know what your daily start times are, correct?"

"Yes, Mr. V, I know what they are."

"And have you been made aware that's it's your responsibility to report to work as scheduled?"

"Yes, Mr. V, I'm aware."

"Ok, then is there anything else that you would like me to know or is there anything that I can do to help you to be on time for work?"

"No Mr. V, I don't think so."

"Would you like the telephone for the Employee Assistance Program?"
"No no no Mr. V."

"Ok, then you may return back to you daily duty."

"Oh, Mr. V, can I talk to my shop steward right now in private?"

"Well, Kwan, since you were late, and the retail window and box sections are backed up, I will permit you time once the mail in the box section gets caught up."

Kwan looked over at Bitsy as if to say, what now Bitsy? Bitsy paying no mind to her, "Kwan check back with me later and I will ask for time for us to talk."

We all walk out of the supervisor's office and resume our routine activities.

0925: "Hey, Reds, who do you think will get Chip's route after he's gone?" asked Zakar.

"Don't you worry about it youngster," replied Reds, "as low as you are on the totem pole you certainly won't get it!"

"Yeah, you're low man!"

"Yeah, a sa la sa lickem brother!"

"Hey, watch it, that's not funny!" shot Zakar.

0940: A postal customer comes to the retail window with a complaint. Her package was received open and missing some of it's contents. Stamped on the package was a message saying Package received in damaged condition or without contents. The customer was concerned that someone had stolen the items inside as well as being concerned about identity theft as there was personal information within the contents. I took her information, apologized, and advised her that I would look into the matter, question her carrier and give her a callback. She asked me how long it would take and when could she expect to hear from me.

"I said ma'am as soon as I can contact the carrier and question him as well as do any necessary research I will then call you back."

She then asks, "Will this be today?"

"Hopefully, yes." I said.

She then said, "Well, I need to know right away. Should I contact my bank since there was sensitive bank information in there?"

"If you think that would make you feel more comfortable then I would suggest you do that, I said." She looked up at me and said, "Ok so you're going to call me today right?" I said, "Yes, as soon as I have information for you." I could tell she was not confident with my answer but nevertheless, we left the conversation at that. Of course, as soon as she left I realized that the employee who had delivered the package was on vacation all week and would not be available for questioning until he came back to work next week. I called the customer back, knowing that she would not be home yet, to let her know of the situation. I apologized and reassured her that I would be in touch.

0951: Phone rings…another customer call…a complaint no doubt.

Ms. Peggy took the call. "Good morning Creeks Bend Post Office Ms. Peggy speaking may I help you?"

The caller had recently mailed a package overseas to China. This was fourteen days ago. Expecting it to be there in five days, the customer had become irritated and was furious. Ms. Peggy asked the gentleman if he had a tracking number, he said: "Yes I do"! She entered the sixteen digit number into the track and confirmation system and found out that his package had been stuck in customs at the domestic overseas postal terminal.

"Of course! Well, how much longer will it be there? The window clerk told me it would only take about five days to arrive at it's destination. Had I known this would have happened I would have used another shipping company, or least a different method of shipping! This is unacceptable." stated the gentleman.

"Well, sir," said Ms. Peggy, I can not tell you for sure but if you give me your name and phone number I will check on it for you and call you back."

He said, "Well, that's what the gentleman told me two days ago and I haven't heard anything yet. I'm not hanging up and no one is going to call me back. He then proceeded to say I want to know now and I'm not going to hang up until I get an answer. By the way," asked the man, "Who is your superior I want to speak to him now?"

"Well, sir my superior is a woman and she is the postmaster," replied Ms. Peggy. He scoffed, "Oh great, another woman! It's not that tall high heel wearing dirty blonde haired lady is it? You know who I'm talking about, the one who doesn't mind showing her boobs. I've dealt with her before she needs to go to Miss Manners school and learn some people skills. Yes, put her hell on the phone right now damnit, I want some answers now!"

Peggy somewhat laughingly choked on his comment and then said, "Sir please do not use that tone and type of language with me."

"Oh, what you have a soft ear do you," he exclaimed.

"No sir I'm just trying to help you and I would appreciate it if you did not swear at me," said Ms. Peggy.

"Okay, "Ms. Softie" listen here, if I were really swearing at you, you certainly would know it, now put Ms. Blondie on before I personally make a trip down there."

Well, she placed the customer on hold and walked into Meghyn's office and explained to her the situation. She also informed her of his anger and language, and his opinion of her. She agreed to talk to the gentleman. To make a long story short, I found out that Meghyn had hung up on this man before because of his attitude and language. Nevertheless, she spoke to the man but to no avail as they got into another heated exchange.

Well, about ten minutes later the same individual called back. Ms. Peggy answered the phone in the usual manner. He was calling to inform us that he was taking his complaint and matter to his local congressman. Peggy simply said, "Ok sir, I'm sorry about your package and the situation." He then rebutted by saying, "You think you heard of going postal…all of you idiots down there will be sorry." He then hung up.

At about 10:15 A.M., I get a call from a carrier whose postal truck has broken down. He's about fifteen minutes from the post office. Apparently, the starter has gone bad so I call the local mechanic whom we have a contract with to tow the truck back to his shop. I then ask the custodian to follow me out to the carrier as I drive a replacement truck out to him. Once there we unload his broken down truck, and reload the substitute truck. Thus he is back on track although he is now about thirty minutes behind schedule.
I go back to the office and finish all of the A.M. paperwork and prepare the next day's schedule. The weekly schedule is already posted but we do a daily schedule every day based on the weekly schedule.

1020: I receive a call from upper management reminding me about a report that should have been submitted twenty minutes ago and is now late. When this happens an email is sent out identify the offices who failed to submit their reports by the time expected. I explained to him the situation with truck breaking and me having to leave the office and she simply says "I know things happen but the next time something like that happens, send somebody else out or make sure you arrange to have someone there to submit the report for you.

Just as I hang up with him, postmaster Meghyn pages me over the intercom.

“Yo V, we’re on the email list for not submitting the ten o’clock report on time, what happened?” she asked.

“Yeah, I know, district just called me. I just sent it…it’s okay.” I reassured her.

“V, I can’t afford to have my name plastered all over the email. Please make sure you stay on top of that. It has got to be submitted on time…okay?”

“Yep, I got cha!”

1022: I get paged to the retail window

“May I have a delivery supervisor to the window? Mr. V, please come to the window.” One of the employees says, “Sounds like another happy customer.” Fortunately, it was a Constable Officer looking for a new address of a postal customer who apparently moved out of town recently and that needed to be served with a subpoena.

1230: Well, it's Friday, and as she is accustomed to doing, postmaster Meghyn leaves work two hours early and heads home. Of course, Ms. Peggy is very happy about that. It's the one day Peggy really looks forward to other than Saturday's, which is Meghyn's day off.

1235: Usually this is when Peggy will get on the phone and call her two little children or log onto the internet and shop. All the employees know her routine.

1300: Chip takes his thirty-minute lunch break. It's at this time that he pulls out one of his click top ink pens and begins to write a note to his daughter Carly on a card he had bought for her last week. Upon completion of the writing he places the card into the envelope it came with, licks it, seals it, and sticks an adhesive "Forever stamp" on it and places it in his "outgoing mail bin" to be mailed with all the other mail he's collected from his route. When he returns back to the post office he will dump the letter into the outgoing letter hamper, along with the other stamped letters he collected that day, so that it will properly receive today's postmark date when it gets processed at the plant tonight. The envelope will bear the postmark date of his last day working at the post office.

1330: His thirty minute lunch break is over and so Chip is on his way back to delivering the mail on his route, for the last time.

1400: Ms. Peggy received a phone call from Lynn. "Good afternoon, Creeks Bend Post Office may I help you?"

"Hello, Ms. Peggy this is Lynn."

"Yes, Ms. Lynn what's going on?"

"I just called to let you know that I will not be able to complete my route in eight hours. Do you have any help you can send me?"

"No Ms. Lynn, I do not have any help I can send you. Besides, I thought you leave on time today Ms. Lynn?"

"Yes, Ms. Peggy, I did."

"Well, then what's the problem? Did you let Mr. V know you might need help today before you left for the street?"

"No, Ms. Peggy I did not. I'm not talking to Mr. V."

"What? Now Ms. Lynn, you know it's your responsibility to notify your supervisor if you are of the opinion you may not be able to complete your route in time or if you're going to need any street assistance. For you to be calling me now is unacceptable. Besides Ms. Lynn, you know that everyone is trying to get done early today so they can go to Chip's retirement party after work. You're just gonna have to get done and get back here Ms. Lynn! I don't have any help to send you."

"Well, whatever Ms. Peggy, I just thought I would call and let you know of my situation. I'll try to make it back in time."

"No Ms. Lynn, don't try honey, I need you back here on time. Can you do that for me?"

"I do my best Ms. Peggy."

"Ms. Lynn honey, your best is not good enough. I need you to do better than your best."

"Again Ms. Peggy, I'll do my best. Goodbye."

As Ms. Peggy was hanging up the phone, with a look of disgust on her face, Spice walked by and asked her…"What's wrong Ms. Peggy, who was that?"

"I can't believe her Ms. Spice! That was Ms. Lynn calling about needing some street help. That she's not going to complete her route on time. Heck Ms. Spice, everyone's hustling today trying to make it back so they can go and get ready for Chip's retirement party tonight. And especially after that stunt she pulled on Wednesday. She's facing major discipline. She should be putting down her better than best performance. She aughtta be racing through that route today. If I were her Ms. Spice I would show management how remorseful I was for my conduct."

"Yeah, well remember who you're talking about Ms. Peggy, some people have no conscious, and she's definitely one of those people, a hussy through and through," said Spice.

"Oh, Ms. Spice I'm afraid you are so right."

"I know I'm right Ms. Peggy! You just gotta call it what it is."

1520: Chip just finished his route and delivery assignments and is now taking his ten minute street break…for the last time. He calls his daughter Carly on his cell phone however, she does not answer so he preceded to her leave a voicemail message. She had been in the shower and then went to lay down to take a nap. As a result, she placed her cell phone on silence and in doing so, did not hear nor feel it vibrating when Chip had called her.

"Hi, Carly this is dad! Well, guess what honey…I'm done, that's it! I have completed my last delivery and am now getting ready to take my last ten-minute street break for good! Wow, this is what it feels like. After all these years I'm finally done! I'm really done and soon I will be clocking out for good! Gosh, I'm so excited and yet at the same time I'm a little bit scared. Gee whiz, what am I gonna do now? Oh, well I suppose you're busy so I will just have to enjoy my elation by myself. Call me when you can, otherwise, I'll see you tonight at my retirement party. I love you, honey, goodbye!"

1550: Phone rings. "Good afternoon, Creeks Bend Post Office Ms. Peggy speaking may I help you?"

"Yes, this is Sgt. Sam Harris from the Creeks Bend Township Police Department may I please speak with the postmaster or whoever is in charge there?"

"I'm sorry Sgt. Harris, but the postmaster is gone for the day. I'm a supervisor, is there something I can help you with?"

"Yes, you may. And I sorry, but what did you say your name was ma'am?"

"My name is Ms. Peggy, I'm the afternoon supervisor here at the post office. Is there something wrong or perhaps something that I may assist you with?"

"Well, Ms. Peggy, unfortunately, I'm calling to inform you that one your mail carrier's was just involved in a vehicle accident. And I'm sorry to inform you but it was a very very serious accident."

"Oh no…how serious was it?"

"I'm terribly sorry ma'am but this was a fatal accident. It involved an employee of your's. I'm sorry to have to tell you this but your employee died in the accident."

"WHAAAT? Wait just a minute sir…did I hear you say that one of our employees was just involved in a vehicle accident, a FATAL vehicle accident?"

"Yes, ma'am, you heard me correctly."

"And you said he died…he's dead…he's literally dead?"

"Yes ma'am."

"Oh no officer please, I can't take this. Please please please tell me it's not true."

"Ma'am I'm sorry, but it's true."

"Oh my goodness! Who was it…can you please tell me who it is?"

"Yes ma'am…the carrier's name is Chip."
"Oh my god! **Oh, my god!** CHIP? **No…no…no,** not Chip…**not Chip!** Oh, my god!"

She took the phone from the one hand and put it into the other hand and lifted it up to the opposite ear as if to hear more clearly. She then placed her other hand on top of her head. Tears immediately started streaming down Ms. Peggy's face.

From what I was told there were some employees in earshot of Peggy's conversation with the officer and so they immediately stopped what they were doing when they heard Peggy scream Chip's name. They knew something terrible had happened based on Peggy's reaction.

"Yes ma'am. I'm so very sorry to inform you of this but we knew he was one of your employees and so I called your office immediately to notify you folks. We all here at the police department have known him for years. This is a very difficult call for me to have made. Ma'am, I'm so very sorry."

From what I was told there was a long pause on Peggy's part…no response.

"Hello, ma'am, are you still there? Hello, again asked the officer?"

"Oh, oh yes officer I'm sorry, I'm here. It's just…it's just that this has totally caught me off guard to say the least. I mean it's like it's not real or something!"

"Yes, ma'am I understand."

"Well, what happened officer, how did the accident occur?"

"According to most witnesses, and of course, we will investigate further, Chip was heading back to the post office and had just entered the intersection with his postal vehicle, as he had a green light, and according to their statements he was broadsided by a lady driving a minivan. Apparently, the lady failed to see that she had a red light and thus drove right through the light into Chip's vehicle striking the truck on the driver's side of the postal vehicle. Sadly to say, all evidence leads us to believe she had been texting on her cell phone.

She obviously was not paying attention. Now the driver directly behind Chip's vehicle said he saw Chip's truck swerve left and right just prior to entering the intersection. I don't know what that's about but we somewhat have two accounts of what occurred. Again, an investigation will need to be done."

"Oh, my…oh my, officer," exclaimed Peggy?

"Yes, ma'am, I know!"

"Well, officer, w-w-w-a-s the lady injured? How is she," asked Ms. Peggy?

"Yes, she did sustain some injuries. She hit her head against the windshield due to the force of the impact. She also sustained some upper body injuries due to her chest hitting the steering wheel. At this point, I would classify her as being in critical but stable condition. Amazingly she wasn't more seriously injured. Apparently, the airbag never deployed. She is being rushed to the hospital as we speak."

"So it wasn't Chip's fault," asked Peggy?

"No ma'am it does not appear to have been his fault. I'm sorry Ms. Peggy but is it possible for you or someone to meet us out here at the scene, preferably a manager?"

"Yes, sir I will be out there as soon as I call the postmaster Ms. Meghyn, my boss, and also notify our District Safety Team. They need to know of this immediately, answered Ms. Peggy."

"Yes, by all means I understand, responded the officer. Do you have a pen and piece of paper to write on? I need to give you the location of the accident as well as my phone number."

"Oh, yes, yes I do have a pen and paper. My hands are shaking but go ahead officer I'm ready." Ms. Peggy said trying to hold herself together.

"Okay, the location is at the intersection of Green Tree Road and Monument Blvd. It's a traffic light intersection. It's less than a mile from the post office."

"Yes, officer I'm familiar with that intersection. I know exactly where that is. I will try to be there in ten minutes but I must make these calls first. However, I will be there as soon as possible."

Upon hanging up the phone, Peggy immediately called postmaster Meghyn and informed her of the situation. Needless to say, the call did not go well. Peggy could barely compose herself. She no doubt was in a state of shock. Spice took the phone from Ms. Peggy and informed Meghyn of the situation based on what she had heard.

"I'm on my way I'm on my way there. Where is Peggy," asked

Meghyn.

"She's right here but I don't think she can talk Meghyn. Her eyes are just staring into space."

"Ok, ok, but I need to speak with her I must talk to her. Please Spice, put Peggy back on the phone."

"Seriously Meghyn, I think she's in shock! She's just sitting here. She's not responding."

"Ok Spice, it's ok, just hang up the phone. I'm on my way."

It was then that Peggy somewhat gained her composure and called me on my cell phone. Upon hanging up with her, I left the funeral home where I was working on paperwork and proceeded to drive to the accident scene.

1600: Meghyn called her boss. Her boss then called her boss. Eventually, headquarters was notified. That's the usual chain of events when an accident occurs, especially with an accident of this nature where a fatality has occurred.

Upon calling her boss and hanging up the phone, Meghyn then attempted to call Mario her boyfriend but her hand and fingers were shaking so badly she missed dialed several times before finally being able to successfully phone him. Mario informed her that he would meet her at the post office as they did not know the exact location because of Peggy's inability to respond.

1610: Chip's cell phone, which had been knocked out of his shirt pocket, landing on the side of the road, rang. But of course, there would be no answering of the phone, as the call went to Chip's voicemail. We found out later that it was Carly, Chip's daughter, returning her father's call. At Chip's burial, she had shared that she had fallen asleep that afternoon when Chip had called her. Upon waking up she had noticed that she had missed his call and that he had left a voice message on her phone. I'm sure Carly would suffer anguish from there on, not only because of his death but also because she had missed his phone call that afternoon…his last phone call.

1630: Because of the direction Mario was coming from, he happened to drive up to the scene of the accident. He immediately phoned Meghyn and directed her to meet him there. I arrive at the scene as well.

1645: Meghyn arrives on the scene. I was told that the coroner's office removal van had arrived at the same time as she did. Because Meghyn and Mario were considered postal officials, they both were let through the blockade and into the taped off accident area. All other traffic was being redirected by emergency personnel from the local fire department.

From what I heard, the postal truck which Chip had driven had been completely crushed in on the postal driver's side. Chip never stood a chance with such an impact. However, we would eventually find out, according to the coroner's report, that Chip had actually suffered a massive stroke which he probably experienced just prior to the accident. For many of us it was somewhat of a comfort knowing that he was already gone before the accident's impact. Hopefully, he never knew what hit him.

1715: All area postal accident officials arrived at the scene. A complete accident investigation was performed on site not only by the police department but the postal safety team as well. All of the outgoing mail that Chip had collected from the customers on his route that day was promptly removed from the truck he was driving and quickly transported back to the post office and placed on the final dispatch truck. Some of the mail had postmark dates for that day on it and therefore had to be processed that evening. Despite such tragedies, the mail must move on. I was also informed that several mail pieces had blood on it and therefore had to be isolated and containerized for safety and public health reasons.

1730: Willie, the office shop steward, sent a chain call out to everyone regarding Chip's accident and death. The retirement party at the Creeks Bend Tavern was obviously canceled. Willie also notified the Tavern where Chip retirement was to take place. The tavern manager understood and was saddened as well. Eventually, the tavern would permanently hang a framed photo of Chip in his memory. Chip was a well respected and much-loved person.

1900: It wasn't until nine o'clock p.m. on that fateful Friday evening that the actual accident investigation came to a conclusion.

There I was, standing, gazing into the west, literally into the end of a setting sun. Since it was summertime it remained daylight longer and so one could faintly see the tail end of the sun setting in the west. And it was then that I remembered what Chip had said during his award acceptance and farewell speech…that he had hopes of spending his retirement years driving into the setting sun. At this point, I began thinking of the song titled "Phone Call to Soliloquy" from the movie "Random Hearts".

CHAPTER **FOUR**

DAY FOUR, Saturday, The Day After

0530: Carly, after having fallen asleep about two in the morning, woke up abruptly to call her father Chip but realized what day it was and that her father was gone. Realizing this, she broke down in tears.

0535: Telephone rings. “Good morning Creeks Bend Post Office may I help you?”

“Mr. V, this is Carly...I’m sorry…I’m sorry to call you at this hour but…”

She paused and then she started to cry. To be quite honest, her call brought tears to my eyes as well. After I gathered myself, because my voice was quivery, I said, “Hello Carly.”

“Mr. V, I’m calling to ask you….”

She started sobbing again, which went on for what seemed to be several minutes. Eventually, she managed to gather herself together and said,

"Mr. V…oh my God I can't do this! First, my mother was taken and now my dad. And my wedding day…I mean how can I get married? This is bulls#*t!"

"Carly…"

"No, no, Mr. V, don't say anything. I can do this, she replied."

Then there was another pause.

"Mr. V, I need to you to…pick up my dad's body."

Then it went silent and Carly started crying again, which again drew tears from my eyes. But we both managed to pull ourselves together.

"I will need you to handle my father's funeral. Can you do that for me…can you do that for him?"

Man, did my throat ever tighten up on me. I mean I could not talk. I felt such heaviness around my chest. Like someone had tied ropes around my rib cage. I felt like I couldn't breathe. All I could do was swallow, swallow hard. The words just would not come out. But eventually, I gathered myself together and assured her that I would take care of her father's body and would handle his funeral arrangements. She thanked me and told me she would call me later on that day once she heard from the coroner office, and then hung up the phone. Wow, what a call. They never trained me for calls like that…I was never schooled on how to handle a call such as a one I received from Carly that morning.

0630: Rico walked through the double doors holding a bible in his right-hand snug against his chest. He proceeds to his mail case. He slowly sat down and said a quick prayer and then began reading his bible.

0650: Up to now, no one had called out sick today. That's a good thing. I really didn't feel like splitting up any routes. Even Chip's route will be covered today because Meghyn had instructed me last night to call in the part timer, Monique, to carry Chip's route.

0655: The seven o'clock transportation truck arrived ten minutes early. Most of the clerk sorted mail has been processed and now we're just waiting to see what's on the last truck. It's shaping up to being a pretty good day mail volume wise. Other than that, there was only this eeriness in the atmosphere. There were none of the typical conversations going on this morning.

0700: All of the carriers, except Lynn and Zakar, started arriving to work early. It's as though they needed to see each other. Everyone was in a state of shock. Rico, Reds, Willie and Old Man are in the swing room. Reds asks the question "How is it that God could let something like this happen, where was He?"

"Yeah, I know." replied Old Man, "As long as I have lived I have never been able to understand him. Why couldn't he have done something?"

Willie chimed in, "I guess he's too busy. What does he care anyway? What you think Rico, you're close to God, I know you got something to say."

"Come on guys listen," started Rico, "this is a very sad and tragic happening, but I don't think we can blame God. As a matter of fact, I know we shouldn't blame God. Yes, God does allow things in this world to happen and I know it's beyond our understanding, but God is not to blame. But personally, since you asked, I think God allows tragedies like this to happen to show us that things in this world are not ok. That something is wrong, terribly wrong, and that things are not right. And I think He allows it to remind us of our human frailty. I think He also allows us to experience these things so that we might seek after Him and question Him, and in questioning Him we might come closer to Him. It's like I said just the other day that its times like these that we really and actually wonder about Him or even talk about Him. It's things like this that get our attention, at least for a while anyway. Don't forget guys, apparently, the lady driving the minivan that hit Chip's truck apparently was not paying attention. According to the reports, she was on her cell phone. Now was that God's fault? No, it wasn't God's fault; it was simply a human failure, human error on her part, not God's part."

"Yeah, Rico, I hear what you're saying," responded Reds, "but look at Chip's daughter. She lost her mother, she's about ready to get married, and now she has lost her father…and tragically!"

"I know Reds," replied Rico, "and I don't have all the answers, but again I believe God allows tragedies to happen to show us that life really is not fair and that there really is something wrong going on here. And it's a good thing that we reach out to Him and ask Him why. I deeply believe He cares."

"Yeah, Rico, maybe you're right?" questioned Old Man, "It does seem like every time there's a tragedy or some horrific event that only then will we ask God where he is. It seems as though we all become sort of religious. Heck, remember 9/11? Everyone seemed to pull together and everywhere you looked there were signs and bumper stickers that read "God Bless America." Eventually, though, that stuff died down and life went on and we eventually went back to our old ways. But I suppose some of us may have changed."

"Well guys look, however, you look at it, you must admit that there is something definitely wrong in this world that we live in. Ultimately you have to ask yourself what's wrong and why…what happened?"

"Yeah, but couldn't he get our attention in some other way?" asked Reds.

"I'm sure He could, but it seems that only through these tragedies God is able to get our attention…at least with some of us. It's like when our bodies are sick and we feel pain or discomfort in them that we realize something is wrong, and that's when we'll seek help through medication or go to the doctors. Well, it's the same thing with life. Unfortunately, most of us will never get it." replied Rico, "We will ignore the pain and continue doing what we do until things get worse and then it's too late. It's the same thing, my friends."

Then Katie, who had walked into the room and heard the conversation and began saying, "Yeah, I hear ya Rico, but I still don't understand God you know! I mean, He just doesn't make sense to me."

Rico replied, "Katie, you have children right?"

"Yes, I have children, so what?!"

"Well, do your children always understand you when you give them instructions or try to help them to see things you already know?"

"Well, no they don't." she replied.

"Right, and do you really expect them to understand you?"

"Ok, Rico I guess I hear what you're saying."

"Well, it's like the same relationship we have with God. If we know that our children can't understand us, how can we expect to understand God? God knows we have trouble understanding Him but all He asks of us is that we trust Him even though we may not understand Him. Isn't that what we want from our children…that they just trust us? They may not understand us but hopefully they will trust us. Come on guys it's not that deep. It may be difficult but it's really not that foreign to us."

“Well, Rico, quibbled Willie, “I guess that’s why they call you the holy man. Personally for me, trusting in someone else is not in me. Especially in someone I can’t see.”

“Willie you don’t trust anyone because you yourself can’t be trusted.” said Old Man.

Rico then replied, “Oh, it’s in you brother Willie…the ability to trust is in everyone. God has given everyone the ability to trust in Him… you just choose not to.”

“Whatever you say, Rico,” replied Willie, “but today is Saturday, Sunday school is tomorrow. I’ll go to church tomorrow.”

“What? You go to church Willie?” asked Katie.

“Yes, of course, I’ll go to church…Bedside Baptist Church and the Pillow Case Choir where Rev. Sheets is the Pastor,” said Willie laughing, as he stood up from his chair and walked over to the coffee machine.

“That’s Willie for ya.” responded Old Man.

That conversation went on for a few more minutes and I noticed, as I looked around, that even Buster was not his usual self. He had casually walked through the doors and quietly sat down at his case. He was quiet and looked reflective. He was just sitting there on his stool with his head hanging down and leaning over the edge of the mail case. *Wow, does it take a tragedy like Chip's to get Buster's attention…to change his behavior, if only for a moment,* I think to myself. Everybody is different this morning. Even Oliver, who does not like to be touched nor will he touch anyone, walked over to Buster and placed his right arm around Buster's shoulder as if to comfort him.

"I know Buster," said Oliver, "I too can't believe Chip is gone. It was only yesterday he gave his retirement speech. He was right here standing among us. He was saying his last goodbye to us, and yet we were all looking forward to going to his retirement party. All those years spent working towards retirement and now nothing. I wonder if his daughter will receive any of his pension? You know Buster, we gotta get out of this place while we're yet able. Life just isn't fair at all. First his wife and now Chip."

Oliver took a hard swallow as if to fight off that choking feeling in his throat.

"What will Carly do?" asked Oliver. "I just can't figure life out Buster."

"I don't know Oliver," replied Buster. Hopefully, he had her as his beneficiary on his life insurance. I hope he had his paperwork in order."

Oliver quickly removed his hand and arm from around Buster's shoulder. I guess it finally dawned on him that he had physically touched someone. Oliver would not touch anyone and Buster would never be found accepting anyone's comfort. It was a strange moment. It felt as though the "Lion had laid down with the lamb." Oliver began to walk away, he repeated…"I just can't figure it out."

0710: Postmaster Meghyn has come in today. She is accompanied by her boyfriend Mario. I'm sure he came to provide moral support for her. She closes the entrance door behind her and proceeds to unlock her office door. With keys clanging, more than usual, she attempts to unlock her office door but her hands are shaking too much. So Mario grabs her right hand to assist her as she pushes the key into the lock and opens the door. The next thing we hear is that familiar sound of the door closing behind her. Normally, it's a sound that most of the employees hate to hear. But today is different. It's a Saturday, and it's the day after Chip's death.

0720: A group of postal officials, including the Letter Carriers Union business manager, along with the District Manager (DM) walk through the doors. I approach them, greet them. I know why they're here. So I walk them over to my desk, pick up the office phone and I call Meghyn on the intercom.

"Hello, answered Meghyn."

"Meghyn!"

"Yes, V?"

"The District Manager is here along with some other postal officials."

"Ok thanks, I'll be right out."

Meghyn opens her office door, walks out onto the workroom floor to greet them, and then escorts them back to her office. I noticed that Mario stood to the side as the DM tensely walked past him. Rumor had it that the DM and Meghyn were, at one time, romantically involved. So there's that opposing male like tension between the two of them. The DM didn't even look as handsome as Mario. However, Mario follows them into Meghyn's office.

0730: The carriers clock in at the time clock. There's none of the usual loud chattering and joking going on. There's just a heaviness of grief in the air. Upon completion of their daily vehicle inspection, the carrier's immediately report to their cases and begin casing up their mail. Chip's case area was vacant. He was not there anymore yet the daily mail was there, daily mail that needed to be cased up and delivered that day. His route had been vacant many times before when he would go on vacation. However, this time Chip would not be coming back. No, not this time. So I put Rico over there to case up the mail and to have the route ready for Monique to deliver when she reports in to work.

0800: Postmaster Meghyn pages me. "V, intercom ten please."

So I proceed to pick up the phone and dial intercom ten. "Yes, Meghyn?" I asked.

"V, just letting you know that the District Manager along with three union representatives, and some other visitors, are preparing to come out to the work floor to address the employees and to see if anyone might be in need some counseling or the EAP. Please have all the employees gather around your desk. We'll be out in a minute."

"Yes, Meghyn," I will, I replied.

0802: Everyone had gathered closely around my desk. Usually, you have to tell them to come closer, but not today. It seemed as though everyone wanted to be close. There was no room for individualism here. It was all about Chip and the unbelievable tragedy that everyone, from the DM to the janitor, has experienced.

Meghyn begins,"Good morning everyone…well, actually it's not such a good morning. She choked up, stopped to gather herself and took a deep breath. "I'm sorry, I don't know if I can do this." She stops again to gather herself. Lifting her right hand to her forehead.,her hands were visibly shaking and her mouth and cheeks were quivering.

Seeing that Meghyn was not in the best frame of mind, the DM stepped in and introduced himself. Though rare, this had not been the first time that the DM had visited our office. In fact, he'd been here twice before. Once, to promote a new product that the Post Office had come out with, and secondly, when Old Man had reached his One Million Mile Safe Driver Achievement and thus was presented with a plaque. Now despite that the DM, on those two positive previous occasions, usually his being there was received with weak acknowledgment and interest from the employees. Most employees and union reps view upper management as waste and evil. Sometimes it's warranted. But to be honest about it, there is waste at all levels of the post office. Hey, what do you expect, it's quasi-government!

However, this particular visit from the DM was received differently and with, if I may say, much welcome. It was like everyone was looking to him for some sort of consolation. As it was, he was the big guy, at the top of the ladder, whom in his forty-one plus year postal career had seen and witnessed it all. So it was that when he spoke, all of us appeared to cling to his every word. All of us that were there that morning needed healing. For a brief moment, both management and craft were united;united in shock, united in disbelief and united in pain. Well, after the DM had finished addressing us it felt as if our office, for that day, belonged to something greater than ourselves. Then and there we truly felt like we were the United States Postal Office. It's amazing how tragedy affects us and brings us all together…at least for a while. But being a funeral director, as well as a postal supervisor, I knew eventually that this sense of togetherness and unity would soon fade away. I'd seen it many times before.

There was a representative from the Employee Assistance Program (EAP) present as well, and so the Local Carrier Union President stepped in to introduce her.

"Hello everyone, this morning we have with us Shelby Morstein. Shelby is from the Employee Assistance Program office. She is here to offer her services to anyone feeling as though they could use some counseling in light of Chip's passing that the Employee Assistance Program is available." He goes on to ask Shelby if she wouldn't mind speaking on some of the counseling resources that are available through EAP…to any who might feel they have such a need.

"Oh, great, a postal shrink. I guess she couldn't get a psyche job in the real world so she turned to the post office!" exclaimed Reds.

"Yeah, Reds, just like you! You couldn't make it out there as a civil engineer so you brought your education into the post office… imagine that!"

"Gentleman, shush!" motioned Willie.

"Thanks, Bill," opened Shelby, "and no I don't mind. First of all my heart goes out to all of you here at the Creeks Bend post office. Unfortunately, yesterday is a day that all of you will never forget. Briefly, I just want you folks to know that the Employee Assistance Program also known as EAP is here for you and anyone who might have the need for counseling or even to just talk to someone regarding…uh, I'm sorry, what was his name?"
"Chip…his name is Chip," said Old Man.

Willie then murmured to Reds, "Geez you think she could have at least known his name…we're nothing but numbers to them people."

"Hey, Willie, now wait a minute. Why is it okay for you people to say them people but it's not okay for us people to say you people?"

"Ha ha ha, very funny Reds…that sounds like that commercial that used to say "Why is it that more than one goose is called geese but more than one moose not called meese?"

Reds just grinned and turned his attention back to Shelby.

"Oh, yes, Chip. I'm so sorry, please forgive me. Well, as I was saying, please know that we at EAP are here to help you get through this very unfortunate situation."

Well, after all of the various postal officials had spoken, we calmly went back to our daily routine, our work…our habitual work. There would be no cake and punch or donuts. This was not a time of celebration, but of only quietness and a time for all to reflect. To reflect on the life we all had known and now was suddenly gone… the life of Chip.

0815: The phone rings. "Good morning, Creeks Bend Post Office, Mr. V speaking, may I help you?"

"Yes, my name is Mrs. Ginnie Temico. I live in the retirement village that one of your carriers served. His name was Chip. We are all shocked out here. Please, can you tell me what happened…what happened to Chip? He was such a gentleman and very dependable. He was a very caring and very sweet man."

"Well, yes ma'am, we all have the same memory of Chip. However, at this time we are not able to discuss or divulge any information regarding the circumstances surrounding the accident and his death…I mean, you know, Chip's passing. I'm so sorry but I hope you can understand."

"Oh, yes, of course, I understand. Well, is there anything that I or we the residents can do for you folks there? We just feel so bad."

"Well, ma'am if you would only send us a card or maybe even some flowers I think the employees here would appreciate that," I responded.

"Oh, but of course, we were going to do that anyhow. I just wish we could do more. Tell me, sir, is there going to be some type of memorial or funeral service held for Chip?" she asked.

"Yes, I'm sure there will be, but at this time we don't have any information. However, if you would like to call back Monday morning I'm sure we will have more details."

"Oh, yes right, it's a bit too early yet to know. I mean it was only yesterday. My gosh, I just can't believe it. None of the residents out here can. We were all up late last night talking about it. Well, anyway I do appreciate your time and I will call back on Monday if that's okay?" she asked.

"Yes ma'am that will be fine."

After that phone call, I reached down into the drawer in my supervisor desk and pulled out the disciplinary paper I was to give to Lynn. With the paper in my hand, I walked over to Lynn and instructed her to come with me into the supervisor's office. She then hollered over to Willie and motioned him to come with her.

"Lynn, please go over to the time clock and swipe over-"

"I know Mr. V, swipe over to operation carrier other, right?"

"Yes, thank you," I replied. "And Willie, please swipe over to union steward time."

"What's up Mr. V…what's the problem?"

I closed the door behind me, "Lynn, this disciplinary Two Week Paper Suspension is being issued to you for the following reasons: **Failure to Follow Instructions and Unacceptable Performance."**

"What!" How is it that I'm being accused of failing to follow instructions and unacceptable performance?"

"Well, for one thing, Lynn, you know that the carrier responsibility manual requires that 'employees are to conduct themselves in a manner that does not reflect negatively on the post office.'"

"Mr. V, this is crazy. You have no evidence that I have done any of this and you have not produced a credible witness. It's all hearsay from some idiot on my route."

"Right, and besides, couldn't this have waited until another day? Gosh, it's the day after Chip's fatal accident!" chided Willie.

"Can you believe this bulls#*t Willie!" shouted Lynn.

"Mr. V, I don't believe you're issuing this…why now? Geez, you haven't even had time to conduct an investigation. Besides, this does not fall into the line of corrective action…it's punitive! How can you go from a PDI to issuing a Two Week suspension in just one day? You didn't even have time to investigate. I mean you say someone called in claiming they saw something but they refused to give their name. Do you have their address so I can go out and interview this so called person?"

"No I don't," I replied.

Lynn started crying.

"Listen, folks, this is being issued for the reasons stated. Willie, here's your copy and Lynn here's yours. Please take a moment to read it and then Lynn I will need you to sign and date indicating that you received it."

"No Lynn, you're not signing anything, just hold onto your copy. I'll take my copy and will fight it. This is ridiculous Mr. V, I mean right after the day of Chip's accident. This could have waited. Don't worry Lynn," continued Willie, "we'll get this thrown out, this will not stick."

Upon that, Lynn threw her copy into the trash can.

I looked at Lynn and asked her, "So you're refusing to sign?"

"What does it look like to you? You heard my union rep! I ain't signing nothing."

"Listen, Lynn," I responded, "if you sign that you received this letter of disciplinary action it does not mean you agree to it or that the charges contained therein are true!"

"Yeah, right Mr. V! I don't trust management in no kind of way, I ain't signing it!"

So with that, I wrote on both my copy and the union rep's copy Refused to sign and I dated it. I was then about to say to Lynn, that Willie and I will meet on this discipline, but she interrupted me and said, "Mr. V, I'm like burger king…have it your way." Turning away, she walked out of the office back towards her carrier case.

"Lynn," I called out to her, "please swipe back into office mode please!"

"What a jerk," I heard her say, referring to me.

I noticed the employees looking over their shoulders at me as I take the familiar route to my desk. I enter into the postmaster's office and placed Lynn's disciplinary letter into her personnel file. Postmaster Meghyn looked at me and said "Can you believe her? She's lucky she's not up for removal after pulling a stunt like that."

I nodded yes and made my way out onto the workroom floor. As I walked out, Willie waved me over to his carrier case and said, "Meghyn put you up to this didn't she?" I just looked at him with a grin.

"You know it's not going to stick Mr. V! You ain't got any witness. I mean it's basically hearsay. Geez V, this is bad on management's part. No wonder craft and management can't see eye to eye. This is not good. The atmosphere around here is already bad enough. You guys treat us like we're animals."

I almost choked on that comment as I turned and walked away.

0900: Most of the carriers, upon the pulling down of their routes and loading their vehicles, began heading out the door to depart to their routes. The atmosphere, unlike other Saturdays, was very quiet. Everyone attended to their work and so the mail was cased up early. Everybody seemed to work at much faster pace. However, just prior to the carriers leaving, I gathered them all, once again, around my desk. I just wanted to make sure that they were focused as much as possible; on their jobs and that they would be safe. They all assured me that they were ok and that they would be back early as they had planned on getting together after work at the Creeks Bend Tavern for drinks. I reminded them again to be safe and to please be sure to change into their personal clothes before going to the tavern. Carriers are not authorized to wear their postal uniforms in public other than to deliver the mail, especially not in a bar.

The day went by fast and without any issues. All the carriers returned back early and safe. Even Lynn had performed her delivery responsibilities without issues that day. Ms. Peggy was happy about that. She actually asked me, "Good heavens V, does it take a tragedy like this to get the carriers to do their job and return back on time?"

"Peggy," I replied, "that's one of the reasons the employees don't like you. I mean I hear what you're saying but I wouldn't let the employees hear you say something like that?"

"Mr. V, you're not here in the evening to deal with these critters, not knowing if they'll make it back in time for the collection truck. I hate having to take the mail to the plant. I have a family at home too just like everybody else."

Then she walked away.

CHAPTER **FIVE**

DAY FIVE, Wednesday, The Day Of

The post office had let employees, those who wanted to; use their lunch break to go to the cemetery to pay their respects. Since Chip was a veteran, a twenty year honorably discharged veteran to be exact, the funeral home had made preparations for there to be a MilitarWedy Honor squad from the U.S. Marine Corps, "Sempre Fidelis, Always Faithful" present at the cemetery. Always faithful, that's what Chip was, right down to his last day.

Once everyone had formally assembled at the gravesite, some sitting but most standing, one of the honor guardsmen, the bugler, began to play the familiar tune, typically rendered, known as "Taps." The bugler stood and played from somewhat of a distance from the site and it seemed as though he were miles away. It was as if the tune had traveled upon the leaves of the trees pushed by the noonday gentle breeze.

Upon the completion of the playing of Taps, two Honor Guardsmen stiffly bent over from the waist, lifted the American Flag that had draped Chip's casket and then meticulously began to fold the flag triangle over triangle until the last six inches of the flag was left and then neatly tucked it into the last fold. It was then that the U.S. Marine detail commander, with the flag in his white gloved hands, approached Chip's daughter, Carly, since she was the next of kin, bowed towards her, whispered his rehearsed speech to her face to face and presented her with the flag. It truly was a solemn moment in time.

The minister began to read from the Bible. He read from the book of Ecclesiastes, chapter three. He began, "To everything, there is a season, and a time for every purpose under the sun…" The minister then proceeded to give the committal. At the end, Carly, somehow, found strength to share a couple of words about her father, and late mother. She really tugged at all of our hearts. We all were swallowing pretty hard.

After everyone had made one final pass by the casket resting upon the lowering device with straps, they said their quiet goodbyes to Carly, and slowly departed from the cemetery, one by one. Eventually, Carly and her fiancé walked back to the limousine. The limo driver opened the rear door to allow them both to enter and then softly closed it behind them. He then walked around to the driver's side door and entered the limo. They were now hidden behind the tinted windows of the limo.

I watched from a distance as the limousine slowly departed the cemetery grounds en route to take them back to Carly's apartment. I, of course, being in my funeral director mode, stayed behind to watch the cemetery workers and to make sure the casket had been lowered properly down into the vault and the lid placed on top. That's what we funeral directors do.

Just like that, it was over. There would be no gathering time of family and friends for the post-funeral luncheon. Nobody was in the mood for that. Besides, the carriers had to get back to work.

Upon the arrival back to Carly's apartment, the mailman greeted her as she stepped out of the limousine, expressed his condolences and then handed Carly the day's mail. It appeared as though she hesitated for a moment but then grabbed the bundle of mail out of postman's hand. Most of the mail consisted of cards and condolences sent from friends, co-workers and postal customers whom Chip had delivered mail to. But she noticed that there was a certain envelope with her father's return address on it. Immediately she dropped all the other cards and mail that were in her hands. It was the letter that he, Chip, had written her the day he died. So with her hands shaking and body trembling, she slowly opened the card and began to lip read…

"My precious Carly, I didn't think I could tell you this in person without my usual tearing up, as you know how emotional I can get. So I thought I would buy a blank card and communicate my thoughts to you this way. Actually, that's how I often did it with your mom. She loved receiving my letters and cards from time to time, accompanied of course, with roses. She said it felt more romantic."

"Your mother and I never held back telling and showing you how much we loved you and how much you meant to us. We always made that a priority every opportunity that we had and I'm glad we did."

"After mom passed away I tried my best to protect you and shelter you from pain as best I could. I'm not sure if that was the right thing to do but I thought it was best at the time. Sweetheart, I'm so proud of you and very much honored to be your father. Despite the fact that I so much look forward to giving you away in marriage I know it's gonna feel somewhat bittersweet. Like I'm losing someone I love, all over again. However, I know that's not the case. Please know that I'm very happy for you and Steven. He is a great guy, kind of like me…just kidding. I also am looking ahead to the day when you call me on the phone to tell me that I'm going to be a grandfather. Oh, look at me. I'm starting to choke up even as I write. Oops, I just dropped a tear on the card. Well, I guess that's a sign that I need to stop writing."

"I will end this letter honey by saying this, even though you are about to experience what should be the happiest day in your life, remember that in this life you will have many challenges, some good and some not so good, as I know you know. But always remember Carly that though the sky may be filled with clouds and the day gloomy the sun is still shining. Ya just have to look beyond the clouds. You know, I don't know why I said that. I suppose I just felt the urge to encourage you…yeah, my famous last words."

"Well, my last lunch break is just about over so I have to go now and finish delivering my route. Love you much Carly!"

"Oh, by the way, I'm glad we chose that style of tuxedo for me to wear. Hopefully, Steven won't mind me looking better than him at the wedding. Hahaha! I love you, honey, ...goodbye...I mean, see you later."

At this point, as I write this story, I hear in my mind Quincy Jones' "Everything Must Change." The message in the song is so true. You should Google it and take a listen when you get a chance.

CHAPTER **SIX**

DAY SIX, Thursday, And I'm Off To Work

0400: I leave home and I'm en route to the Post Office. Guess who is in front of me? Yup, you guessed it…the guy who drives twenty miles per hour in a forty-five mile an hour speed zone. As usual, he is taking his own sweet time, as if there's no one else in the world but him. Once we reach the area where it's safe to pass, I do so.

0425: I arrive at the Post Office, pull into my usual parking spot. As I said earlier, everything we do in the Post Office is repetitive and monotonous. It's a habitual job and we basically do everything the same way every day. I guess that's the one thing about this job that employees like, there's basically no change. People don't like change.

0430: I clock into work at the time clock. Bitsy, Pudgy, and Samantha are there performing their typical daily tasks. Since it's Thursday, Samantha is in on her scheduled day off so she is happy… it's all time and a half pay for her.

0645: I hear the clicking of high heels, keys jingling and the unlocking of the postmaster's office door, it's Meghyn. *Oh boy here* *we go, back to the usual grind.* I quickly get up from my seat and head to the men's room.

0700: Like clockwork, Rico arrives and walks through the doors with his lunch bag and a bible in hand. Per his daily routine he proceeds directly to the break room to eat his breakfast and read his bible.

0717: Meghyn walks out of her office onto the workroom floor, "Good morning Bitsy…good morning ladies!

"Good morning Meghyn." they all said simultaneously.

"Hey, where's V at?"

"You know where he is Meghyn. answered Pudgy.

"Oh yeah, of course, he's in the men's room! How's the mail flow today?" asked Meghyn.

"Well, it could be better but we're getting there. Just need to finish up the letters, they are heavy today. And then we'll get to these parcels." Bitsy sighed.

"Hey, Samantha, how about you move over here and help Pudgy throw these letters. Bitsy, you stay on parcels." ordered Meghyn.

It's then that I exit the men's room and walk out onto the workroom floor. Meghyn sees me and asks, “Yo V, where is Katie? It’s seven eighteen! She should have been here by now! Where is she?” asked Meghyn.

As I get ready to pick up the phone to call Katie on her cell phone, I hear the beep sound of a time card swiping through the time clock.

“Oh, there she is! Katie…remember…seven fifteen seven fifteen not seven eighteen!” exclaimed Meghyn.

“I’m sorry boss! Traffic was sluggish this morning. There was an accident about five miles from here.” she said as she casually walked towards us.

“Come on Katie,” shouted Meghyn, “get a move on it, we don’t have all day! I want you to help scan these parcels!”

“Yes, ma’am on the double,” replied Katie!

I heard Bitsy mumble, “Yeah, right on the double. Imagine her working on the double. Boy, I can’t wait to retire and get out of this place.”

“I here ya Bitsy,” I responded.

Meghyn swished her head around and rolled her eyes at me and quietly said, “Not now V, but later on I want you to give Katie a PDI…enough with the official discussions bit I want discipline issued! You got me?"

"Si senorita," I said as I nodded to say yes. She gave me that trademark grin as she walked past. I turn to Spice, who was standing nearby and overheard the conversation, "Meghyn's the only person I know who will deliver a death sentence with a smile."

0725: The carriers are standing at the time clock getting ready to clock in. Buster, bursting through the doors loud and boisterous as usual, saw Lynn standing at the time clock waiting to swipe in along with the other employees. Without missing a beat "Hey, Lynn, what time do you wanna get together for lunch today?…drop your drawls…I'M OUT!"

Lynn retorted, "You are such a black butt hole."

Buster turned towards Willie and started laughing!

Oliver put his hands up to his mouth as in disbelief to what he just heard.

"Well, you can tell it's back to work and business as usual," said Bitsy to Samantha.

"Yeah, I hear ya Bitsy," replied Samantha. "It is what it is and at the end of the day, everything is everything!"

THE END

www.ingramcontent.com/pod-product-compliance
Lightning Source LLC
Chambersburg PA
CBHW060248100426
42742CB00011B/1677

* 9 7 8 1 9 4 2 7 0 5 4 3 7 *